Endors

The Way reminds us of the extent to which our current very serious geo-political, societal, and environmental issues are the result of our own thinking and failure to look beyond the needs and demands of ego. Our ability to manage these growing dangers with wisdom, cooperation, collaboration for the sake of mankind will depend on our ability to transcend our immediate desires and access our more enlightened and compassionate selves. *The Way* offers time-tested suggestions for how to do this. Provocative, enlightening, and highly readable, *The Way* provides a unique perspective on our troubled times.

— Lynn S. Paine, John G. McLean Professor
and Senior Associate Dean for International
Development at Harvard Business School

How do we live a loving and meaningful life in a world that has become so derailed? How can we contribute to its transformation in positive ways? To understand this, we must first gain insight into ourselves. We are connected to the world—and live with much stress, anger, frustration and pain in our daily lives; we expend much negative energy. *The Way: Finding Peace in Turbulent Times* offers us guidance to confront all this in constructive ways, leading us to a greater inner harmony.

This volume is not a simple 'self-help' book, nor is it a sermon from on high. With a point of departure in the wisdom from many ancient traditions—but angled to our contemporary realities—and with the addition of an array of insightful modern perspectives, Sankey and Lockwood speak to us as wise and compassionate friends. They unpack our deep-rooted everyday dilemmas, shed light on their origins, and point to concrete patterns of thought and action that we can take, with the help of practical exercises and experiments.

The text is sprinkled with wise and evocative quotes, not only from the traditional and modern spiritual leaders and philosophers, but also from diverse figures such as Freud, Einstein, and A. A. Milne (author of *Winnie-the-Pooh*). The authors bring out the common threads that unite this broad chorus of voices—and show how they all indicate paths towards greater self-insight and well-being.

Highly recommended!

—Peter Dahlgren, Professor Emeritus, Sweden

It is often said that education turns a mirror into a window. What *The Way: Finding Peace in Turbulent Times* does is to turn the mirror into a window into the soul, allowing us to discover who we really are underneath all that veneer of ego-derived conditioning. As we un-peel the layers and delve into ourselves, we discover the secrets of living in a way that substantially reduces, if not eliminates, the stress and suffering of our life. We then find that most of the so-called 'problems' we face are essentially self-induced, a product of our egocentric mind for which we are entirely responsible but which we do not know how to address.

Peace cannot be found by seeking to change the external circumstances of our life. Our life will be what it will be, and we will inevitably confront all manner of events. Peace will be found, and can only be found, internally, inside each of us, in the way we think and the way we manage our thoughts. We already have everything we need to resolve the issues. We simply need to learn how. This book explains in practical ways how to truly understand who we are and the techniques for managing life and finding Inner Peace and Harmony.

—Professor Rosario Drago, Instructor in Marketing,
Villanova University, Pennsylvania, USA

The Way: Finding Peace in Turbulent Times is a fascinating and inspiring book which takes *The Stairway to Happiness* to new levels. It is profound and thought-provoking and takes the reader on a journey of intense self-discovery in order to access the secrets to finding serenity and peace. By discovering who we really are, deep down, which is not the ego-derived sense of self that we might like to think we are, we create an objective space in which to observe our thoughts and behaviours which then allows us to make whatever changes we need. As we develop an awareness of what really matters in life and learn to master negative thought patterns by accepting, rather than fighting, 'what is', we effectively transcend ego and discover a place of peace and joy to which we can return at any time.

The teachings contained in the book date back thousands of years and are inspired by the wisdom of the many sages whose extraordinary insights and sacrifices have inspired billions of people across the ages. These teachings are complemented by the scientific thoughts of spiritual luminaries such as Albert Einstein and Max Planck. In *The Way: Finding Peace in Turbulent Times*, science meets spirituality.

—Claire Howell, Chief Executive and
Senior Executive Coach of REDCO Ltd

We are living in a world which seems, at times, to be insane. Just look at the news at any time and contemplate the state of the world. There are injustices everywhere and we prefer to spend vast sums on vanity projects rather than use those funds for the benefit of our planet, the natural world that sustain us, and those who need our help most. There are enough resources in the world to eliminate hunger altogether, yet the greed of a few make this an unnecessarily difficult task.

The ability to think, the unique gift of human beings, has evolved to the point where its capacity to do good is now exceeded by its capacity to destroy itself. Human beings need to evolve to a new state of consciousness that transcends these dangers and to do it rapidly before it is too late.

The Way: Finding Peace in Turbulent Times, which applies teachings that date back many thousands of years, exposes the issues facing mankind today and provides a way forward, which involves nothing less than a transformation of thought. This transformation is a rediscovery of who we really are underneath the thick layer of conditioning that we have inherited and continue to create. The irony is that we already have everything we need to save our planet and our species. It is a simply a question of re-discovering it. This book makes fascinating reading.

—Martin Hatcher, former Executive Chairman,
ScanSource Communications Ltd and MTV Telecoms

The Way: Finding Peace in Turbulent Times has been a real gift for me and a springboard for change and inspiration, as well as a most enjoyable read. On re-reading it a second time I found its teachings even more profound. It has caused me to reflect deeply and absorb its uplifting messages which resonate so clearly with me and often take me back to periods in my life which were left too far behind. I am very grateful to have had the opportunity to read this book, which I recommend highly. Thank you, Vernon and Katey.

—Dr Bart Debruijn, Medical Doctor and
Senior Advisor and Counsel

My family and I really enjoyed reading *The Stairway to Happiness* and looked forward very much to reading Vernon's next book, co-written with Katey Lockwood, *The Way: Finding Peace in Turbulent Times*. It has been another remarkably insightful, thought-provoking and uplifting experience, taking the messages of the first book to entirely new levels and the reader to deeper levels of understanding. The point is well made that humanity needs to change the way it thinks if we are to survive as a species, and this book shows clearly how this can and should be achieved. We also love the poem, 'When We Awaken', which features in the book. We feel particularly attached to it because Vernon shared it with us as it was being written.

—Jeff Kay, former Chairman and Founder of the Quadrant Group

Sankey and Lockwood integrate a dazzling array of thinkers into their work, *The Way: Finding Peace in Turbulent Times* and synthesize these thoughts in a straightforward manner. Readers who implement these ideas into their spiritual life will find the calming nature of the tome most encouraging. A great read.

—Dr Elliott Drago, History Department Chair, Central High School, Philadelphia, Pennsylvania, USA

THE WAY

Finding Peace in Turbulent Times

VERNON SANKEY and KATEY LOCKWOOD

Improve Your World

ISBN: 978-1-9995972-3-8 (softcover)
ISBN: 978-1-9995972-4-5 (Kindle)
ISBN: 978-1-9995972-5-2 (EPUB)

Improve Your World Publishers Co Limited
www.improvemyworld.com

Book design by Jill Ronsley, Sun Editing & Book Design, suneditwrite.com

Printed and bound in the United Kingdom

The mind can go
in a thousand directions,
but on this beautiful path,
I walk in peace.

It is my conviction
that there is no way to peace.
Peace is the way.

—Thich Nhat Hanh

Contents

Acknowledgments

> The first thing we have to say respecting what are called new views here in New England, at the present time, is, that they are not new, but the very oldest of thoughts cast into the mould of these new times.
>
> —Ralph Waldo Emerson, lecture January 1842

Our first acknowledgement is to the very many sages, thinkers, philosophers, prophets, writers and spiritual teachers of the past, whose genius has had such an influence on the writers and the writing of this book.

As Ralph Waldo Emerson so correctly states, 'new thoughts' are often very old thoughts adapted to the different circumstances of a different age. This is certainly the case with this book. Here some of the very oldest thoughts have been re-presented in order to enable today's readers to access the immensely valuable teachings of the Ancients.

These thoughts (some dating back over three thousand years) have not only stood the test of time but are also so relevant to today. This is testament to their enduring and spiritual quality and value. They may have sometimes disappeared from public view and appreciation in the intervening years, but they are now again being discussed, written about and adopted by increasing numbers of people, as the collective awareness that we must change the way we think grows ever more prevalent.

The difference between our 'new times' and Ralph Waldo Emerson's is that these thoughts have now taken on an importance to the survival of mankind that would have been unimaginable earlier.

The destructive power of medical, military and technological science is now such that the world could be annihilated. It would take just a handful of determined, untransformed, evil-minded people. Moreover, our own selfish actions and our inability to understand the lessons of the past have resulted in increased and evident dangers to our world: pollution; global warming; unacceptable disparities in standards of living; the destruction of vital animal and plant species; and continuous human conflicts. We seem to be hell-bent on destroying ourselves, even as we all profess to be mature, thinking adults who recognize the risk!

It is time for human beings to awaken. We must realize that something must be done to return the world to a place of greater safety and peace and to provide all future generations with a decent life on a decent planet. This may seem like some sort of utopian dream, but it is possible. Millions want it to be possible. And if we fail, the nightmarish consequences—the result of our own irresponsibility—will be final.

The idea of awakening to a new way of thinking arose some two and half thousand years ago! Independently and in different parts of the world, but interestingly at approximately the same time, there arose a new class of philosophers, sages and thinkers. They spoke and wrote about the soul and a new way of thinking. That way of thinking was about living such that the soul was placed at the centre of existence, aligned with a universal force that underpinned all life.

This universal force was all that had ever existed and would ever exist in the universe and beyond. It was beyond human understanding and ineffable. It was without form and could not be named or categorized since to do so with human verbal concepts would destroy its meaning.

Living in alignment with this universal force meant living with respect for the world and all its creatures, in a compassionate spirit of non-violence and kindness, in tune with nature and virtuously. It meant understanding the meaning of life and learning how to transcend our mortal body to a higher plane and awaken to a higher consciousness and inner peace. Above all, it meant understanding our innate egoistic nature and learning to master it.

These thinkers lived around 500 BC and included in India the Buddha, Krishna and Veda-Vyasa as well as the founder of the Jain religion, Mahavira, Zoroaster in Persia, Lao Tzu in China, the pre-Socratic philosophers such as Pythagoras and Heraclitus in Greece, and Hermes Trismegistus in Egypt. All these sages proposed broadly similar ideas of goodness, ethical behaviour, justice, tolerance and forgiveness. Unlike organized, institutionalized beliefs and religions, they did not prescribe rules and regulations, but advocated a deep understanding of the formless nature of universal love, which transcends human understanding and focuses on the enlightenment of the eternal soul.

That these ideas are still so applicable today is because of their timeless, vital, living quality. These thinkers knew that 'religions' would rapidly deteriorate into dogma, rights and wrongs and believers and blasphemers. They were showing us ways in which to live in conscious alignment and harmony with goodness and eternal truth. It was about understanding the connection to soul rather than to man's inadequate systematic dependence on limited knowledge and logic.

Albert Einstein, a scientist but, more importantly, a deeply spiritual thinker, said of this:

> The scientist's religious feeling takes the form of a rapturous amazement at the harmony of natural law, which reveals an intelligence of such superiority, that, compared to it, all the systematic thinking and acting of human beings is an utterly irrelevant reflection. This feeling is the guiding principle of his life and work, insofar as he succeeds in keeping himself from the shackles of selfish desire. It is beyond question closely akin to that which possessed the religious geniuses of all ages.

Many of the ideas expressed by these wise sages *deliberately* have no 'form'. They defy description because they are beyond human understanding and thus cannot be categorized in human terms. They are expressions of eternity and eternal perfection. This divine perfection is already in us—if we can learn to discover, or more accurately rediscover, it in ourselves.

We *can* sense the power in the sages' words because *our own* power is contained in them. They are all pointing to the way of self-discovery, truth, love and inner peace.

It is to all these immortal enlightened teachers and ascended masters that this book owes its primary thanks and we would like to acknowledge the immense and immeasurable brilliance of the teaching that they brought to the world.

Since that time, there have been many other great sages, prophets and wise people, such as Jesus of Nazareth and Muhammad, whose teachings have been along similar lines and have influenced the lives of millions. Many have lived in contradiction with the culture of their time and been murdered for their cause. They have died in the name of peace.

More recently, writers, thinkers and scientists have created books, articles and treatises of great quality about these 'old' ideas and brought them to life in many different ways. We acknowledge the role played by many of these authors and thinkers who have stimulated our imagination.

They include such luminaries as Carl Jung, Albert Einstein, Max Planck, Viktor Frankl, Dan Millman, David Hawkins, Wayne Dyer, Eckhart Tolle, Deepak Chopra, Norma Milanovich and Shirley McCune, James Allen, the 'Three Initiates', Karuna Cayton and the many translators of ancient texts. Their inspired thoughts have helped us to gain a wide understanding of the various possible interpretations of the ancient wisdom and enabled us to form our own view as expressed in *The Way*.

We are especially indebted to both our families and many friends for the encouragement, support, tolerance and patience as well as their many suggestions, improvements and contributions. Creating a book such as this takes many hours—time that cannot be spent on other activities. Debbie Jaarsma, Casper Jaarsma, Bud and Elliott Drago, Jeff and Sue Kay deserve special mention for their wonderful help and creative suggestions to our work.

Elizabeth Sankey (Vernon's wife) listened and contributed to what sometimes seemed like interminable discussion, debate and reflection over the significance of different points throughout the writing process. Without her selfless love, understanding, kindness and perception, this book could not have been written.

Katey would like to acknowledge her Nan who has been a constant and inspirational support on her life journey. She has been a wonderful source of encouragement to her, not least with her studies of philosophy, the Kabbalah, energetic healing and other wisdoms.

Katey would also like to pay tribute to her Mum, Sharon, for her constant support, encouragement and loving kindness as well as so generously giving of her time. It was Sharon who gave Katey her first sense of spirituality when, as a small child, she cradled her in her arms and sang: 'You are everything and everything is you.'

Many thanks are also due to our editor, Jill Ronsley, for her enthusiasm, advice, suggestions, brilliant attention to detail and sheer competence. It is always a delight to work with her.

Introduction

If you have picked up this book and are reading it, it is no coincidence. It means you are awakening to an inner realization that a radically new way of thinking is needed if we are to reverse the catastrophic journey on which humanity is travelling. You will be conscious of a profound disquiet within your soul and an intense sense of frustration about your apparent helplessness at the state of the world. You can see that we are heading for very turbulent times but are very uncertain about what we—or more precisely *you*—can do about it.

The world's increasingly complex and confusing problems—conflicts, inequalities, environmental destruction and a frenetic pace of change—have given rise to fear, anger, resentment and deep anxiety. Although there are wonderful initiatives and selfless acts happening around the world every day, they are constantly overwhelmed in the media by the torrent of bad news. The disharmony and divisiveness felt within and between nations, generations, creeds and genders, the intensification of work demands, the anxiety about the future direction of technology are all causing a pandemic of stress.

The very existence of so much negativity repeatedly bombarding our subconscious mind burrows into our brain. Since 'what we think, we become', this creates a perception that the world is an unfriendly and dangerous place. This leaves us perpetuating a vicious cycle of negative thoughts. We then start to believe that while the dangers in the world are intensifying, few practical solutions exist to address these issues. There seems to be nowhere to go for respite. The world is out of control.

> Only when the last tree has been cut down, the last fish caught, the last river poisoned, only then will we realize that you cannot eat money.
>
> —Native American saying

There is a crisis of leadership. Leaders are narrowly focused on short-term, parochial 'hits' designed for quick wins and re-election, rather than on the wider good of society—let alone mankind. Few genuinely awakened or transformed leaders are emerging. Our leaders are failing to provide the statesmanship, considerate direction and collaboration that is a prerequisite for solving today's immensely complex global problems. Rather they often fuel the fire of dissent, fear and anxiety with heated and divisive rhetoric. While this may win votes in the short term, it is an unwise and ultimately self-defeating strategy that can only work against world peace.

What is needed is for a new enlightened, broad-minded and compassionate class of leader to emerge. Their aim, and the aim of their electors, should be to create a world that respects all its inhabitants (whatever their preferences and backgrounds), that protects the natural habitat and environment on which we all depend, and that lives in harmony and peace on a planet we all share. Their most important task, however, is to encourage, promote and model a change in the way we all think. We have to move from egoic, self-centred individuals, bent on getting all we can irrespective of the consequences, to human and spiritual beings who realise the interdependence of all living creatures and the absolute need for working collaboratively in a spirit of compassion and kindness.

On an increasingly crowded planet, we can only survive by evolving our state of consciousness to a level that will enable us to address the problems we face. We can only act at the level of consciousness we have. If we want to resolve more complex challenges, we must do this by raising our consciousness to a higher level. It is the mission of this book to explain what this means and how to achieve it.

The current negativity, the conflicts and suffering that permeate our daily life—hardly a day goes by without news of some appalling act of hate and divisiveness—is utterly insane. A visitor to our planet would think we are truly pathologically and criminally insane in how we are treating each other and our world. There is no need for any of it. It achieves nothing. It is also entirely avoidable.

> No tree has branches so foolish as to fight amongst themselves.
>
> —Native American proverb

The Way to Finding Peace in Turbulent Times is intended to help readers understand how negative thoughts, fears and anxieties arise and how to deal with them. The way we think as individuals affects the collective mind and determines the fate of the world itself. Unless we change the way we think individually and collectively, nothing will change. The world will continue down an increasingly dangerous and calamitous path. This is not idle fear-mongering but the conclusion of many erudite thinkers, scientists and philosophers, some of whom are quoted in this book.

> The public is still in denial about two kinds of threats: harm that we're causing collectively to the biosphere and threats that stem from the greater vulnerability of our interconnected world to error or terror induced by individuals or small groups. Moreover, what's new in this century is that a catastrophe will resonate globally ... In our networked world, there would be nowhere to hide from the consequences of economic collapse, a pandemic, or a collapse in global food supplies. And there are global threats; for instance intense fires after a nuclear exchange could create a persistent 'nuclear winter' ... In such a predicament it is collective intelligence that would be crucial.
>
> —Martin Rees, Astronomer Royal, *On the Future: Prospects for Humanity*

Collective intelligence, collaboration and cooperation—the prerequisites of creating a new, safer and healthier world—can only begin when enough people learn to think differently and use their power to radically alter the course of history. There is a solution to every problem if we learn to use our immensely powerful minds in a different way. We have to master our ego and thought processes and remind ourselves who we truly are, where we came from and where we are going. The solution to all our problems lies within our own souls and our desire to do what is right for our world, for our environment and for humanity. True peace is within us already. All we have to do is remove the conditioning that obstructs the light from illuminating this truth.

> But above all you should understand that there can never be peace between nations until there is first known that true peace which is within the souls of men.
>
> —Black Elk

Understanding how we think, where these thoughts are generated and how to control them radically alters the way we look at life itself. It allows us to dissolve negative emotions such as anger and resentment and convert them into more positive outcomes, which contagiously attracts other benefits, often described as synchronicities. Mastering how we think is *the* key to living a more harmonious and happier life and attaining a state of inner peace.

Inner peace is a mental discipline that allows us to become the observer of our thoughts, to be consciously aware of who we are and, equally importantly, who we are not. Through self-awareness, we awaken to our ego-free presence. Inner peace is about rising above negative thinking and detaching ourselves from the conditioning and beliefs that we have acquired—from parents, peers and society—and finding the stillness within us.

The only constant in life is change. Life throws up challenges and that is entirely normal. The human condition is by nature unstable and unpredictable. The way we think determines how we view and deal with these challenges. We can either bemoan our lot, blame other people and fight the events that happen—causing ourselves frustrations, anger and pain—or we can deal with them in a positive way, accepting full responsibility for our actions and recognising that challenges are there to help us learn and evolve.

Evolution is the result of overcoming difficulties. Every time we encounter an event or a person that presents a challenge and we address them positively and from a position of inner calm, we build internal power. We should never give that power away to anyone else or allow other people or situations to control our thoughts and actions. If we feel anger or resentment at the actions of another, we are effectively handing control of our emotions to someone else. By living in the truth of who we are and not someone else's perspective of who they might like us to be, we remain masters of our soul.

Our human journey—this ultimate game of life—is our opportunity to do good and serve others. Keeping our morals high when others behave badly, accepting and forgiving, gaining strength in adversity and being grateful for all we have—these are all expressions of goodness. They stem from our awakening from the unreal dream of ego that we have learnt to master. Ego is the principal cause of our dysfunctional behaviour, anxiety and stress. It follows us in darkness. Mastering it is a lesson of *The Way*. It is *the Way* to inner peace.

> I came out alone on my way to my tryst.
> But who is it that follows me in the silent dark?
> I move aside to avoid his presence, but I escape him not.
> He makes the dust rise from the earth with his swagger; he adds his loud voice to every word that I utter.
> He is my own little self, my lord, he knows no shame; but I am ashamed to come to thy door in his company.

—Rabindranath Tagore, 'Who Is This?' from *Gitanjali: Song Offerings*

In *The Way*, we refer regularly to the Universe. We sometimes call this force God but, more often, we refer to this indescribable force as eternal light, universal intelligence and several other terms. Avoid associating these words with any religion or religious image you might have. Using an ambiguous term that is difficult for us to associate with a specific idea or image is deliberate, as the concept of universal power goes way beyond human understanding. Words are wholly inadequate to explain this intelligence of such magnitude.

We are all part of this universal intelligence and we are all interconnected whether we like it or not. What anyone does anywhere in the world is reflected everywhere. All that we see around us reflects our thoughts and is the product of our mind—from the most beautiful and inspired to the most dangerous and destructive. If we suffer so many conflicts and have amassed so many weapons, it is the direct result of our fears about the intentions of others. If we have unprecedented levels of pollution, it is the result of our collective greed and desire for things at the lowest cost possible without regard to their human or environmental impact. If we truly cared for our planet, we would be more conscious of the effects of our actions and behave differently. Our outer world is always a reflection of our inner world. What we think is what we create. We are wholly responsible for the state of the world we live in. It is the direct product of our thinking and the actions that ensue from that thinking. In the words attributed to Hermes Trismegistus two thousand years ago: 'As above so below, as below so above.'

By working on managing our *inner* world, we can improve our *outer* world. It is the only possible way to achieve this and to live in a safer, happier, more peaceful world.

> ...the more we tame the aggression and conflict within our own being, the more we are able to attend to the needs of our community. Inner peace truly is the path to world peace. This doesn't mean we stop working to make things better and change the harmful conditions in the world, but we need to do so from a mindset and inner motivation of empathy, compassion and peace. As Mahatma Gandhi so aptly said, 'An eye for an eye leaves the whole world blind.'
>
> —Karuna Cayton, *The Misleading Mind*

In writing this book and rediscovering the way to inner peace, we have studied and reflected on works that date back many thousands of years. These include Hermetic, Egyptian, Vedic, Jewish, Indian, Persian, Chinese, Buddhist, Christian and pre-Socratic texts, philosophies, religions and ways of life, as well as those of philosophers, scientists and spiritual teachers right up to the present day. It is remarkable to note the close philosophical similarities between all these teachings—not least the existence of universal love or God, the path to conscious awareness, awakening to divinity, enlightenment and the role of acceptance, inclusiveness, kindness, compassion, forgiveness and love. Although living in different parts of the world and at different times, these philosophers, sages and thinkers arrived at very similar conclusions.

Unfortunately, many of the teachings then became corrupted by man-made dogmas and the human need to organize and control. Once these beautiful thoughts become incorporated into a belief system, ideology, political credo or religious cult, they become rigid and lose their essence. They become the *only* true way. Other interpretations are wrong. Strict rules and regulations are introduced. There is a right and wrong way. The concept of believers and unbelievers appears. At this point, the entire original idea of openness, inclusiveness, acceptance and love is shattered. It is swallowed up by the ego-based desire to control others and to demand obedience. The spiritual dimension of Oneness is lost in the human dimension of duality. The pure message of *absolute* love is lost to *relative* human perceptions of right and wrong, good and bad, love and hate.

Universal love cannot be defined and has no need of any definition. It encompasses everything. It is formless, infinite and perfect. Being perfect, it is itself and complete. It is one. This is Oneness.

Universal love or Oneness is everywhere and there is no place where it is not. Although we like to think we are in some way separate and different—which paradoxically is the cause of so much pain, suffering and conflict as our ego tries to prove how unique and different we are—we are always part of one ubiquitous Universe. And if it is everywhere, it must logically also be in us, should we choose to see it. This is part of the journey of self-discovery and inner peace.

Universal love is consciousness. It is who we are before we allow our ego to seek to make us different, better, right, wealthier, more fashionable, more 'successful', in competition with others and needing their approval. Until we understand this, we will continue to live a life of duality—where there is always instability and conflict and where we can never find lasting inner peace. The jewel of our true essence cannot be found outside us in the world of duality, things and forms. It can only be found inside, in the unseen, formless, unconditioned consciousness of our Being.

> My eyesight is clear now, yet the jewel is nowhere to be found. I look upon the valley far below, where I began my climb many years ago. Only then do I realize that the jewel had always been within me, even then, and that the light had always shined. Only my eyes had been closed.
>
> —Dan Millman, *Way of the Peaceful Warrior*

The Way to Finding Peace in Turbulent Times seeks to explain all we have raised in this introduction.

Part 1 presents the reader with seven key learnings to begin the process of radically changing the way we think. This includes specific actions and recommendations.

Part 2 provides more depth and detail behind the ideas and philosophies expressed. It considers principles and universal laws that govern life. It contains several exercises and practices.

Part 3 summarises the critical challenges facing humanity and offers solutions at both the individual and collective level.

The Universe needs you. It wants you to see and experience the immense power that you possess when you awaken to your consciousness. It wants you to help, guide and inspire others on this, our human journey towards a higher, more spiritual dimension. Only by raising our level of consciousness can we address and solve the immense problems that we—or more correctly our egos—have created.

It is gratifying to see a different attitude not only in the younger generations but also across all generations. The awakening process is evidently well underway. Ideas that were considered 'weird' and 'way out' not long ago are now seen as increasingly mainstream, not least as science continues to substantiate them. Many people now see the dangers that we face in their true light, and they want to make a difference to their world, their future and the future of their children. We can become the creators of a better world as we evolve to a higher level of consciousness.

We hope you will see this book as a gift of learning, as a springboard for change and as an inspiration to make our world a better place. It comes with a heartfelt message of love, gratitude and peace.

And the wind whispered…
'They are not listening still'
And my heart cried out from the wilderness,
And tears welled in my eyes…
And the wind whispered…
'Be at peace child…
They are listening,
They have heard,
They are coming,
They have perceived paradise.'
And the peace came…
And eased the pain.

We hope this book will help you find your truth and your wisdom.

PART 1

The Principle *of* Inner Peace

1

Introduction to the Seven Key Learnings

Have you ever felt completely still and at peace with yourself, irrespective of what is going on around you and the circumstances of your life?

Have you ever sensed that there is an energy source within you that seems to be working independently of your physical body or your mental thoughts and yet is definitely present?

Have you ever wondered in awe at some beautiful scene, a piece of music or a natural phenomenon and felt an inner glow of joy even before you consciously recognized and gave a name to whatever it was you perceived?

Have you ever said to yourself that it doesn't really matter what happens since every event that occurs, whether positive or negative, is really just an opportunity to learn, grow and acquire wisdom?

Have you observed how making judgments about things, people or situations creates duality (good-bad; helpful-obstructive; exciting-dull), division, resentment, conflict, whereas accepting what is, as it is and for what it is, releases tension and reduces stress?

Have you experienced negative thoughts in yourself and others and realized how this unbalances your inner peace and poisons the atmosphere, let alone how we feel physically inside?

Part 1 'The Principle of Inner Peace' examines and applies the wisdom that has come to us from the past, in many cases several thousand years ago, to enable us to awaken to a new way of thinking. This way of thinking transcends our human condition. It is essentially spiritual yet remains totally relevant to today and essential to the world's future well-being.

The scientific community was originally very critical of this wisdom, since it could not be 'proved', yet it, too, has gradually started to discover evidence for concepts previously felt to be fanciful and absurd. Today, science's most creative and emancipated minds, in all branches including medicine, are increasingly accepting and adopting many of these ancient practices.

In Part 1, the key messages about how to handle the stress and anxiety of living in today's hectic world and *enjoy a calm, serene life in a state of inner peace* are outlined. If we change the way we think and return to our original state of Oneness, we will not only significantly improve the way we feel about ourselves and our world, but we will also change the world itself and make it a better, safer, friendlier place for future generations.

The following chapters cover the seven key learnings that allow us to return to a state of inner peace:

1. **Oneness—You are not alone** (being part of one Universe; understanding ownership and attachment and detachment)
2. **Acceptance, Surrender, Positive Thinking and Living Now** (also responsibility, letting go and trusting the Universe)

3. **Eliminating Negative Thinking and Judgment** (as well as limiting beliefs)
4. **Forgiveness, Compassion, Kindness, Morality**
5. **Gratitude, Awe, Enthusiasm, Joy, Appreciation**
6. **Stillness, Self and Purpose**
7. **Living a New Way of Life**

Before coming to these learnings, it is important to understand and embrace some essential, practical preconditions. If we want to find inner peace, everything that we do in our life must aim to come from a place of love and non-judgment. We cannot give love to others unless we are able to love ourselves. 'Loving ourselves' means to live with our actions and behaviours, knowing that they come from a place of kindness and acceptance and knowing that this is how we are trying to live our life. *We can only give what we have.*

If we do not have love for ourselves, we have no love to give to anyone else. If we feel bad about who we think we are and what we think we need, want or are entitled to, then we cannot love ourselves. All we will have to give is negativity in the form of judgment, resentment, envy, anger or fear.

With this mindset, we cannot re-discover the inner peace that is our essence and is in us already but hidden behind this thick curtain of negative thoughts and feelings. Nor can we create a more peaceful and happier world if we are constantly sending out negative messages into the Universe, which are then picked up and multiplied by similarly negatively inclined people. We end up with a dangerous, greedy and polluted world. A world where image is more important than substance, where lying is more rewarding than telling the truth, where the accumulation of things is preferable to the beauty of simplicity and nature, this is the sort of world we have created. To change this to a more virtuous cycle, we have to clean out the toxins of negativity first.

To start the process, we need to take care of and respect our bodies, not for reasons of vanity, but out of respect for the life we are privileged to have been given. If we abuse our bodies through excessive, unhealthy eating, drinking, smoking, lack of exercise, hydration, or sleep and compulsive stress, we are demonstrating physically our absence of love for ourselves. This promotes pain, suffering and unhappiness and adds a thick layer of difficulty between us and the calm serenity we want.

It seems obvious and common sense to write this but having a healthy, balanced diet, keeping a healthy weight, drinking plenty of water, not smoking, not taking substances, drinking little alcohol, taking aerobic and strength exercise, avoiding excessive caffeine, getting seven to nine hours' sleep a day are all obvious actions to take and they work symbiotically with each other.

The greatest contributor to bad health, however, is stress. Stress instils a sense of despair, provokes panic attacks, irritability, fatigue, as well as headaches and muscle pains. Stress releases cortisol, which destroys essential gut bacteria. Their loss results in food intolerance, weight imbalance, skin deterioration, stomach disturbances, autoimmune conditions, fatigue and poor sleep. It is a major cause of high blood pressure, heart disease, strokes, type 2 diabetes and cancer. While mentally, it results in intense suffering and pain and affects not only the sufferer but also all those around him or her.

The world is experiencing an epidemic of stress, which is clearly extremely damaging. It harms not only individuals but also the Universe, since it promotes pessimistic thinking and negative, low-level vibrations. It is the cause of so many of the mindless conflicts and seemingly irrational decisions that we witness at the geopolitical level every day. It results in rash, imprudent decisions that put the entire world at risk. It harms relationships and blocks peaceful co-existence and harmony. Ironically, it is all entirely avoidable. It does not have to be like that.

Stress is purely a product of our thoughts. Our thinking determines the level of stress we experience and our ensuing emotions. There is nothing obligatory about stress. It need not exist. It is a construct of our ego. It is unreal. It is an illusion that we mistakenly believe to be true. When our mind is overwhelmed by negative thoughts and feels unable to cope, the result is always stress. A mind that thinks it cannot cope becomes unbalanced, disharmonious and confused.

Stress is not the same as hard work. Hard work is never stressful to the person who loves what they are doing. Stress is not evident when life is being lived without resentment, anger, fear or coercion or when there is no expectation—either negative (retribution) or positive (recognition). When living is an adventure not an ordeal and there is an attitude of awe and wonder, curiosity, inspiration and enthusiasm, there is no stress. There is just joy and contentment.

The answer to managing stress and living a life of inner peace lies in the way we think. Everything is the product of our thinking. There is nothing outside of us that can help us achieve this. It can only be achieved by changing internally. Only if we change our thinking, can we eliminate stress and change our life.

2

Oneness—You Are Not Alone

The way to self-discovery and inner peace begins with the realization and understanding that we are not separate beings. We are not isolated and alone, but part of a beautiful and infinite Universe from which we came and to which we will return.

The Universe is itself in perfect balance and harmony. It is all energy, and everything is connected to everything else in a giant and expanding energetic matrix. We are part of that infinite energetic source. This all-powerful source exists because of an indescribable, unimaginable and infinite power that is present and can be experienced easily enough.

Our bodies are composed of billions of cells, most of which replace themselves on a continuous basis. The physical body we inhabit today is very different from the one we inhabited a few years ago. Yet we still maintain our ability to think, we have memories and we are the same psychic person that we were before. Our physical body may have changed, but our soul, which is an emanation of universal consciousness, who we are, is still intact.

Universal consciousness has been called by many names, God, infinite light, divine spirit, Oneness, and so on, none of which do it justice. Being formless and infinite, with no beginning and no end, it cannot be described in words, which are forms and thus wholly inadequate. 'To name it is to lose it!' as is said of the Tao. Or in the words of Alan Watts: 'You can't get wet from the word "water"!' Giving something a name doesn't mean you can experience it. All we know is that this Spirit, source or force 'passes all understanding' in its power and capability and clearly exists.

It is encouraging and illuminating to note the extent to which deep-thinking scientists have come to appreciate and accept the existence of this universal and creative consciousness.

This is what Max Planck, very much a left-brained analyser and scientist, the winner of the Nobel Prize for Physics and after whom Germany's premier scientific institution is named, said about the existence of a universal intelligence:

> All matter originates and exists only by virtue of a force which brings the particle of an atom to vibration and holds this most minute solar system of the atom together.... We must assume behind this force the existence of a conscious and intelligent mind. This mind is the matrix of all matter.
>
> —Max Planck, 'The Nature of Matter'
> (speech given in Florence, 1944)

What was understood over 2,500 years ago by ancient civilisations and recorded in Vedic, Hermetic and Chinese texts and reflected in magnificent architectural, astronomical, artistic and philosophical achievements was, with the advent of certain organised religions, subsequently denied for many hundreds of years. These same religions, we should remind ourselves, asserted that the world was flat and the sun went around the earth, which was the centre of the universe. Ironically, this same scepticism also pervaded scientific beliefs until relatively recent times. Only now have advances in science, and especially psychology and quantum physics, begun to validate what ancient sages had known all along but could not 'prove'. With every new discovery, modern science, which is only some four hundred years old and hence in its infancy, recognizes the enormity of what it still *does not understand* and has yet to discover. Science acknowledges the presence and power of a universal force or intelligence even though it cannot explain it, any more than it can explain what a 'thought' is made of or exactly where 'memories' reside. Albert Einstein recognized this same spiritual power when he formulated his law of relativity and began to unravel the mysteries of particle physics.

> Everyone who is seriously involved in the pursuit of science becomes convinced that a spirit is manifest in the laws of the universe—a spirit vastly superior to that of man, and one in the face of which we with our modest powers must feel humble. In this way the pursuit of science leads to a religious feeling of a special sort, which is indeed quite different from the religiosity of someone more naïve.
>
> —Albert Einstein

The founder of analytical psychology Carl Jung felt a similar powerful force: 'I could not say I believe. I know! I have had the experience of being gripped by something that is stronger than myself, something that people call God.'

What is the relevance of these insights to finding inner peace? By recognizing that we are not separate, solitary beings having to fight our own way to survive but connected to a universal intelligence means we are an intricate part of something much larger than ourselves. There exists something much more significant, meaningful and collectively good than the normal sense of separation and isolation. Feeling separate means feeling different. Feeling different means feeling superior or inferior. Feeling superior or inferior are ego-based thoughts that create conflict (I feel superior so I must be 'better' than you or I am inferior and thus resentful or envious of you). And creating conflict means creating division, hate, pain and suffering—the antithesis of inner peace!

The billions of cells that make up our body are unaware of the existence of each other. Yet they all function naturally, in perfect harmony, to support, protect and heal the whole body, of which they are a part. If a cell changes and breaks this harmony, the body becomes dis-eased and sick. The cell loses its alignment with the whole and, if not corrected, can corrupt and kill the whole body.

In the same way, the billions of people on earth, most of whom will never know more than a few others, are also part of the whole of humanity and connected to the Universe. The earth and everything that lives on earth, all the planets, stars and galaxies are all also part of one Universe and one intelligence, held together in a perfect matrix of energy. If we choose, due to our egos or our leaders', to think we are separate, and thus better than or fearful of others, then we too create dis-harmony and risk poisoning the whole, with catastrophic results. If we are all connected, we are all metaphorically part of one body. If we are part of one body, we need to do all we can to ensure that we work harmoniously together. Why would we voluntarily choose to damage any part of it? Why would we want to harm our own selves? It makes no sense, other than to our ego, which thrives on conflict, difference, fear, anger, anxiety and stress.

When we recognize this, and the fact that what powers us and provides our being is the energy of the Universe—since everything is energy and vibration—then it follows that we too are powered by that same energy source, which is our soul or spirit, a microcosm of this Oneness.

> Spirit is the essence of consciousness, the energy of the universe that creates all things. Each one of us is a part of that spirit—a divine entity. So the spirit is the higher self, the eternal being that lives with us.
>
> —Shakti Gawain

We came from this divine spirit in the first place. This is who we really are. We are spirit and we are soul.

> Never tell a child you have a soul. Teach him, you are a soul; you have a body.
>
> —George MacDonald

Possibly the most appropriate description of this unimaginable force is infinite love. These two words enable us to try to conceptualize at least some of its enormity without using a word such as 'God' that evokes too many preconceived notions.

We are all part of that infinite love, which is itself the very embodiment of inner peace, a peace that we all inherently possess. All we have to do is re-discover it within ourselves. It is already there. It is not outside of us. Most of our religions recognize this, but the understanding goes back thousands of years. We can see it in the Tao of Taoism, the Noble Eightfold Path of Buddhism and the 'heaven within' referred to in Egyptian and Hermetic texts. Plato calls this inner treasure of life 'the good and beautiful', while more recently certain African people have used the concept *ubuntu*. To take another example, the Shinto religion (Shinto means 'the path of the gods') in Okinawa, every person is considered to have an essence called *mabui*. All these words point towards the same source of our soul or spirit. It is immortal and is who we are.

> The Kingdom of Heaven is within you; and whoever shall know himself shall find it.
>
> —The Agrapha, the non-canonical sayings of Jesus

> For behold, the kingdom of God is within you.
>
> —Luke 17:21

> I entered into the innermost part of myself.... I entered, and I saw my soul's eye and unchangeable light shining above this eye of my soul and above my mind.... He who knows truth knows that light, and he who knows that light knows eternity. Love knows it.
>
> —Augustine of Hippo, *Confessions*

Unfortunately, what has happened is that we cover up our internal light and connection to universal love with beliefs, conditioning and the negative, divisive thinking of our ego. The sun is still shining brightly but we cannot see it because of the clouds and storms that we have created. Heaven is within every one of us. We are primarily spiritual beings, temporarily housed in a human body. In a paraphrase of Hegel's thought: We are not human beings on a spiritual journey, we are spiritual beings on a human journey.

When we see this, we realize that we came from a limitless, kind, inclusive Source. We are also inherently like that, that is who we are and need to rediscover in ourselves. Once we understand this, all our everyday worries and the stresses and strains of our transient physical life cease to have such importance to us.

When we let go of events, people or situations that, in our ignorance, we perceive negatively, and take a more objective view of them from a point of higher awareness, we immediately reduce their negative impact and make them easier to deal with. In the context of universal history, they are just a blip. They really don't matter and certainly don't deserve to cause us such stress, suffering and unhappiness. By letting them go and seeing them in perspective, we re-establish a quiet mind that is no longer fighting and in conflict with itself. We can then reconnect with eternal gentleness.

> The memory of God comes to the quiet mind. It cannot come where there is conflict, for a mind at war against itself remembers not eternal gentleness.
>
> —*A Course in Miracles*

Inner peace is gained by understanding our essential and infinite spirituality that transcends all mortal matters. It makes our temporary human incarnation—a mere dot in the context of history, the hyphen between our dates of birth and death—much less significant.

When you know you are part of this divine source, which accompanies you everywhere and is always with you, you need no longer fear anything, even death. When your mortal body dies, you simply go back to the source from which you came.

If you realize that all things change,
there is nothing you will try to hold on to.
If you are not afraid of dying,
there is nothing you cannot achieve.

—Stephen Mitchell, *Tao Te Ching: A New English Version*

'Love is God, and to die means that I, a particle of love, shall return to the general and eternal source.'

—Leo Tolstoy, *War and Peace*

Where is thy sting, O death?
Grave! Where thy victory?
The clod may sleep in dust beneath,
The spirit will be free!

—John Bowring

We can remove the obstacles to inner peace by getting them into perspective. We can develop a sense of detachment from things, events, beliefs, money, being 'right', even people. From a very early age, human beings have a habit of wanting to 'own' things and forming attachments to them. Because we often see ourselves as separate, a function of our ego encouraging us to be superior, we allow our possessions, titles, life story, beliefs and how other people describe us to define us and to make us feel different.

Soon after we learn the word 'I' we learn the words 'me' and 'mine'. This is *my* toy and later *my* house, *my* car, *my* partner, *my* career, which leads to *my* reputation, *my* beliefs, *my* entitlement, and ultimately *my* life. These are all ego-based and simply feed our egoistic sense of self—an unreal fantasy that can only cause pain and unhappiness. Yet we form deep attachments to these labels because our ego and vanity encourage us to think this way.

We then start to believe that these illusions are not only part of who we are but that they *are* us. We associate ourselves with them and they become our sense of self. This attachment can be very powerful and all-consuming, even if entirely illusory. 'I have this title and these possessions,' we think. 'Therefore, I'm better, wiser, more important and attractive, more everything than you and I am different from you.' Similarly, we hold that 'These are my beliefs, and they are more profound and better founded than yours,' which creates conflict and closes the door to learning anything new. If we think we already know, we cannot be taught anything.

This type of thinking is doomed to failure. Yet we all have aspects of this attachment syndrome and it begins at an early age. Ask a small child to give his or her favourite toy away to another child to see the strength of attachment! We adults are no different. This ego-based desire to own and to be attached to things, 'our' ideas and to winning—which means others must lose—takes us into a continuous conflict zone and further and further away from infinite love. Our natural state of inner peace will remain inaccessible when covered by such a blanket of egoism.

Possessions, our beliefs and even the people we know and love are transient and thus inherently unstable. They cannot last forever. They will disappear. Sometimes it will take many years and sometimes it is very rapid. But disappear they will. We may lose our job or reputation. Our house may burn down. Our possessions may be taken. Our partner may leave for another. People die.

Forming strong attachments to objects, money, reputation, the past, being right and to people is a recipe for suffering and pain, especially when it is the product of ego desire. When an ego-based attachment, which has become part of who we think we are, disappears or dies, then part of us also inevitably dies.

In some cases, the suffering and pain is so traumatic that people never recover from their loss. During financial crises or periods of great uncertainty, the suicide rate goes up. When reputations are shattered, health is frequently severely damaged. When sports people come to the end of their playing careers, they often experience a deep depression. When children fail to meet up to the images they see on social media or are ostracized by their friends their mental health deteriorates dramatically. In all cases, they have become so closely attached to the image their ego has created of themselves that when that image is shattered, they too shatter.

However, this pain and suffering is wholly understandable and appropriate in the case of the loss of people whom we love and who are very close to us. This love is an emanation of infinite love and is pure and unconditional. This is not an ego-based attachment, with its craving for control, power over others and selfish desires. On the contrary, this type of attachment is entirely selfless. It never tries to control, judge or seek anything for itself. Rather it respects people, without precondition, for who they are and with *all* their characteristics. This type of attachment is pure. It is untouched and untouchable by ego. It is wholly aligned to universal consciousness. It is love.

Love is not, though, ownership. Ownership is meaningless. In reality, we never own anything. We may have temporary use of something, but it will either deteriorate and disappear or someone else will take over its use. Whatever it may say in the contract, we will only have the use of something for a limited period of time. What is the point of developing any attachment to such ephemeral stuff?

The reason for the advice to reduce the attachments we have for the objects and the people we care about in our life needs to be properly understood. It seems to run counter to the desire to love unconditionally, which would result in being wholly attached to our loved ones. This is not a call for indifference, cold-heartedness or any diminishing of the deep feelings of love that are part of our physical and spiritual being and totally aligned with infinite love.

On the contrary, it is a call for discernment between what is really important and what is purely trivial. We should ensure we always take the time to truly appreciate that which has true spiritual value and emanates from love, truth and kindness. At the same time, we should realize that all human things are ephemeral. They change and dissolve. They are ultimately unreal, since only the things that do not change—the soul and universal love—are real and changeless.

Precisely because we know that people are transient and cannot last forever, we should take every opportunity to cherish and enjoy, with unconditional love and total selflessness, all those whom we hold in deep affection. We should never take them for granted or not make time for them. One of the greatest regrets anyone can have is realizing when it is too late that time has been spent and wasted on feeding the ego and on trivialities when that time could have been spent on higher-order activities: loving, caring and nurturing in the service of goodness.

We should also learn to let go at the right time and detach ourselves when it is appropriate to do so. Children will leave home. They need to live their own life and not be held back by parents whose loving attachment can become, for egoistic reasons, a barrier. Children should be allowed, as soon as is practical, to make their own decisions, learn from their own mistakes and live their own life. We can guide them but telling them what to do does them no favours. Friends, too, will move on and we should help them to find the life they want. If we truly care for our employees, we should accept that their futures may be best served by moving to another company. Careers need to end so that the next generations can take over. Leaders need to know when it is time to go and not overstay their tenure.

> Sharpen a blade too much
> and its edge will soon be lost …
> Retire when the work is done; this is the way of heaven.
>
> —Lao Tzu, Tao Te Ching

We need to use the life we have been given to the best of our ability—doing good, finding our calling and serving others. This non-attachment to earthly things, this letting go, this surrender to what the Universe, in its absolute wisdom, has decided should happen anyway, is a foundation of inner peace.

Our mortal and fleeting existence should always be comforted by the knowledge that our soul is eternal. It has no attachments and no need of them, since we are connected to infinite love.

The words 'it doesn't really matter' or 'it is what it is' are indicative of non-attachment and surrender. They are not intended as some cynical, dejected comment on the meaninglessness of life. Rather they are a realization that, in the grand scheme of things, many of the events that upset our inner peace are purely ego-based and, therefore, *do not matter at all.*

By recognizing this simple fact, we awaken to the truth that we take everything, and especially ourselves, much too seriously and need to view life in a broader, less self-centred, less stressful way. The reason the Buddha is often pictured with a smile on his face is that he is mildly amused by the totally unnecessary suffering that we inflict on ourselves by the self-importance that we project. Nobody has the right to think so highly of themselves. There is something comical about those who seek to project such arrogance. What really *does matter* is our individual and collective spirituality. We have to free ourselves from the chains that bind us to our ego-based attachment to possessions and ideas that are the cause of such suffering and pain. Removing the negative conditioning of our ego will always allow us to regain our original state of inner peace.

According to a Sufi fable, the phrase 'This too will pass' was etched on a ring given to a Persian king who asked his sages to give him something that would make him happy when he was sad and help him regain a state of peace when he was anxious. The sages decided the inscription on the ring would always remind him that everything is transient: the bad will become good again, the rain will give way to sunshine, the storm will pass. The only constant is change. In the words attributed to Friedrich von Schiller:

> Let not thy heart cling to the things which for so short a time deck out thy life.

3

Acceptance, Surrender, Positive Thinking and Living Now

Everything is constantly in a state of flux and unpredictable. We have little real control over most of the things that affect us and the problems we encounter. Yet we continually fight to try to gain control. This leads to frustration, anger and stress as our ego is thwarted. Inner peace evaporates. In order to maintain our sense of self, we respond by complaining. We are suffering from bad luck; other people are behaving badly and are to blame; the world is (always) against us; life was so much better in earlier times; and so on. Everything is responsible except us, of course. Maybe, just maybe, might we be responsible?

Could it be that our need to control, to bring about the solutions we desire irrespective of the effect on others and our attempts to control the uncontrollable is at fault? Until we accept responsibility for everything that happens in our life—and this means *everything*—we will be a victim and not a victor of our circumstances. We will hand power and our ability to find happiness and fulfilment to whoever we blame for our predicament, our anger, our fear and our stress. Until we accept that we cannot and should not seek to control everything, that we should accept those things that lie outside our control and surrender our power to universal love, which is always perfect and in harmony, our suffering will continue to increase, and inner peace will elude us.

Inner peace can never be achieved in a mental state that agonizingly tries to control and solve everything itself and blames everyone else when failure inevitably occurs. If we try to control outcomes, which are dependent on others, rather than controlling our own thoughts and actions, we will always be frustrated and stressed.

In the words of Woody Allen: 'If you want to make God laugh, tell him your plans.'

What we can control

The reality is that we can only control two things: our own thoughts and our own actions in the moment—right now. And it's gone. Right now again. And it's gone. Everything else is either in the past and we cannot change that. Or it's in the future, which is always by definition uncertain and volatile. While we can have some influence over what may happen in the future by our current actions, we cannot determine the actions of others or, most importantly, decide the outcome or fix the future. Attempting to do so is futile and only leads to anxiety and suffering as we agonize over whether something will or will not happen.

If we try to live the future now, which is an impossibility, we remain anxious and, even more seriously, fail to live our life the only way we can, which is right now. When we try to live the future now, we cannot concentrate on what we are *actually* doing. We end up devoting the time we should be spending enjoying our life on anxieties and fears about the future. When we should be resting we are having sleepless nights, as we mull over all the terrible things that might happen.

The only time the future can be lived 'now' is when its 'now' eventually comes about. Otherwise, we are wasting time inventing possibilities based on fantasy fears.

If we can only control our own thoughts and actions and cannot control anything else, how should we deal with all those events and happenings that lie outside our sphere of control and live in a state of peace?

There are many aspects of our existence that we need to understand in order to learn how best to handle life's challenges in a calm and stress-free way.

The first truth that we must accept and surrender to—and, therefore, not try to fight—is that life is constantly changing.

> Everything changes and nothing stands still.
>
> —Heraclitus

Life is therefore also always unstable and unpredictable and will evade any attempt we may make to exercise control over it. As a result, we have to learn to deal with an endless stream of unstable and evolving issues every day of every year. That is the nature of human existence. It will always be so. The key questions are: How do we tackle these challenges? And how should we best organize our thinking, since how we think will determine how we react?

Problems or challenges? Perception or reality?

If we think that challenges are negative events or problems that bombard us and that we have to find ways to fight and win battles in order to overcome them, then we will live a life of continuous conflict and stress. In such a life, inner peace will be impossible to achieve. If, on the other hand, we embrace challenges and learn to view them as opportunities to learn, then our mindset is more likely to produce positive and happier outcomes.

There is no such thing as a problem. 'Problems' are always opportunities to learn—as are our 'failures'. They enable us to understand what does not work and lead us to an understanding of what does work. They teach us about ourselves. They show us what we are lacking, what we need to understand better. They are pointers to what we can improve. Making mistakes is a wonderful way to learn and develop—nearly always the very best way.

> Failure is the true test of greatness.
>
> —Herman Melville

However, it does require us to draw the lessons from the challenges we have faced. If we do not learn the lessons and understand what—in us, not externally—needs to change, we are condemned to repeat the same mistakes. People often complain that they keep on getting the same results over and over. If they are in an abusive or conflict-ridden relationship, they may leave it only to find their next one has the same characteristics. If they are in a job they do not like because they do not feel appreciated, they leave it only to find they land in another one where they again feel unappreciated.

They then conclude that everybody is selfish and unkind. This negative perspective cannot result in inner peace.

What we have to do is to develop different thinking. We need to take the time to stop and think through carefully what is going on in our own mind. We need to become the observers of our thoughts, giving us distance, and deliberately examine where these thoughts and the feelings they give rise to are coming from.

What is it, in ourselves, that is creating the results that we are attracting? Why are we making the choices that we are making? What expectations do we have and why do we have them? Are they ego-based? Do we 'want' or 'need' something that may satisfy our ego but is not aligned with universal love? Do we associate ourselves with our image of the job or the perfect partner or relationship without understanding that our image and expectations are a function of our ego? Do we worry about what other people think of us and give undue attention to pleasing others irrespective of our self-respect? Have we not heard the saying: 'What others think of me is none of my business?'

> Healing comes only from that which leads the patient beyond himself and beyond his entanglements with ego.
>
> —Carl Jung

If ego is driving our decisions and choices, then we will always end up with unhappiness and disquiet. We cannot return to a state of inner peace if our actions are motivated by the cravings of our ego. Nothing can *ever* satisfy our ego for long. If we don't get what we want, we are unhappy. And if we do get what we want, we experience happiness, but only for a very short moment, and then we soon become unhappy again. The ego will always want more. It is never satisfied.

Whenever we find ourselves viewing challenges negatively, it is always because our own mental perception of the issue is a negative one and the product of our ego. It is our mind, and our mind only, which is transforming the issue into a problem. The issue itself is almost always neutral and it has no intention of harming us. In many instances it is often also an illusion and unreal and exists only as a figment of our imagination, created by the limited beliefs, prejudices, fears and the desires of our ego. Ego is wonderfully efficient in enlarging any negative disproportionately, making a proverbial mole hill into a mountain. Or, in the witty remark attributed to Mark Twain: 'I've lived through some terrible things in my life, some of which actually happened.'

It is our own internal perception of every situation and our own state of inner peace that can either create or dissolve our anxiety. Changing our perception of any situation will reduce its negative impact. If we no longer consider it a problem, but an opportunity, we will have a more positive perception and will be better able to handle it. When there are no problems that cannot be resolved and turned to advantage, we can live (again) in peace and calm.

> Men are disturbed, not by things, but by principles and notions which they form concerning things.
>
> —Epictetus

By raising our mindset to one that sees positives rather than negatives, accepts rather than blames, and seeks to satisfy what is good and pure rather than the cravings of ego, we are adopting a more spiritual approach. And then there is always a spiritual solution to everything. However, when we take a different and more positive view of things, we have to ensure that it is our spiritual being that is leading our mind and not our ego or false sense of self. If we practise this spiritual approach so that it becomes the way we are and the way we live, we will always change the outcome to a more favourable one. Wayne Dyer's well-known quote expresses this in a way that also evokes the 'observer effect' in quantum mechanics and particle physics, whereby the mere observation of quantum phenomena or electrons changes them.

> When you change the way you look at things, the things you look at change.
>
> —Wayne Dyer

There is nothing that cannot be achieved when we truly believe that it is possible and we turn our mind to it. What we focus on expands and if we think only positively, and discard doubt, and our efforts are directed at doing good and serving others, we will inevitably attract extraordinary results as there is nothing that cannot be accomplished.

> 'Very truly I tell you, whoever believes in me will do the works I have been doing, and they will do even greater things than these...'
>
> —John 14:12

Sometimes these will seem to be like little miracles—often the consequence of the bountiful synchronicities that we are attracting from the Universe. Everything is possible. This is the attitude that creates in us a state of inner peace.

> If a man could pass through Paradise in a dream, and have a flower presented to him as a pledge that his soul had really been there, and if he found that flower in his hand when he awoke—Ay! and what then?
>
> —Samuel Taylor Coleridge

Accepting what is

Another important way to deal with the problems and suffering that we encounter and return to a state of equanimity is to accept 'what is'. This means to accept each situation as it happens, without trying to fight it. Trying to fight what is will always be a source of stress because our ego's idea of what should or should not happen will either not occur or be the result of stressful exertion. Accepting what is is an expression of humility. It is not for us to try to control others or external events or to presume that *our* plans are the only plans that should prevail or are more important than others'. It will be the Universe that will decide anyway.

When we learn to accept what is for what it truly is, without wishing to change it, we change our mindset. We go from fighting, resistance, being 'in charge' and being 'right' to acceptance and surrender. In a state of surrender, the mind has nothing to fight against and becomes calmer. We are then in a much better condition to handle whatever comes our way. Acting from a state of surrender is not passive because the actions that ensue from this state of peace have an energy that affects everything we do. That sense of peace is consciousness itself. It can never depend on what is outside, only on what is inside us. What is outside is uncontrollable. What is inside is entirely in our hands, or rather our minds, and that is where the secret of finding stillness and peace is found.

Accepting what is does not mean that we should be prepared to accept acts of unkindness, cruelty, bad behaviour or anything that is contrary to what is aligned to divine goodness. If we are not comfortable with what is happening, we have to take responsibility to act in accordance with what is right. Not doing so means not taking responsibility for our state of consciousness, since we would remain dis-comforted and unaligned.

When we are confronted with a difficult, negative situation, we should do all we can to remedy the problem. If the bad behaviour is directed at us, then it is always wisest, if we have been unsuccessful in defusing the situation, to simply walk away and not allow ourselves to be provoked. Similarly, we should take the people we seek to protect out of harm's way. Responding to anger and hate with anger and hate means that our ego is now engaged, which can only result in conflict, pain and suffering—even violence. By engaging our ego, we are allowing ourselves to behave in exactly the same way as the other party. This will resolve nothing and most likely make things worse. Not retaliating, not allowing ourselves to become embroiled and not allowing our ego to take over are difficult aspects to master. They are essential tools that require training. As with martial arts, the real skill is not in striking but in avoiding, deflecting and overcoming by peaceful means.

When I (Vernon) was training for my black belt in Tae Kwon Do, in one of the less wealthy areas of Norwich, we would often go to the local pub after the session. Our Korean teachers were extremely talented, even though they were not big and did not look particularly strong. On one occasion, a fight broke out between two men at another table. They took their disagreement outside but kept bumping into the door, which would knock into the table we were sitting at. One of our teachers, Mr Lee, a world martial art champion and former police detective, felt the need to stop the fight. He went outside with his hands in his pockets and said in broken English, 'No good. No fight. Stop now.' The locals were not impressed that this 'foreigner', who was much smaller than they were, was telling them what to do and so they temporarily stopped their own quarrel and turned on him. They tried to punch him again and again. Hands still in pockets, he deftly stepped out of their way. He was so much faster that they could not strike him. Nor could they get a grip on him physically. He was simply too quick. After a while, the two men looked at each other and realized that something odd was happening. And as quickly as it had started, the fight was over. They stopped, turned and walked away. Mr Lee, whose capacity for doing damage was immense, had not had to use violence at all. The lesson he had shown was one of restraint, of mind and ego control, of peace.

Accepting 'what is' is about addressing all those other things that irritate, anger, frustrate and upset us. It is our ego that tells us we 'deserve better', we should not put up with something and the world is there to serve us. It is the ego that expects 'perfection'.

Not long ago, I (Vernon) landed in the US after a long flight, only to be confronted by a huge queue at immigration control. Two or three large planes had landed just before us and the poorly air-conditioned hall had over a thousand people. There was an audible groan as passengers, some with small children, realized the wait they would have to endure. The frustration levels increased and complaints could soon be heard. Some became angry and argued with the officials who controlled the lines. The negativity was palpable. Who wants to stand in line for nearly two hours after a long flight?

My options were either to join in the complaints, which were pointless and would only satisfy the ego for a very short time and then attract more negativity, or to accept the situation—the what is—about which I could do nothing anyway.

I chose to go into my own mind and soul, in a state of calm, and began a mild form of meditation. It included being exceedingly grateful for all the wonderful things in my life, of which there are so many, for being on a visit to the US, an amazing country with wonderful people, and having the privilege of doing something I loved with people I respected and really enjoyed being with in what I knew would be a beautiful location....

Before I knew it, I was at the front of the queue. I had to look for my passport as it was not, as with so many other people, already in my hand. As I came to the desk, I smiled at the officer and said hello and he smiled back. I was pleased to see him and glad of his response. He took my passport, looked through it and said, 'You seem to have come zillions of times to the US. Why are you coming this time?' I told him I was coming to give a presentation and a workshop. 'What about?' he asked, out of genuine curiosity. I told him. He then said: 'That's a wonderful subject. I'm really interested in that. Where can I find out more?' I told him I had written a book. He immediately handed me a piece of paper and asked me to write down the name of the book as he wanted to get it. He then stood up, handed me back my passport and said, 'So nice to talk with you and with someone so happy and relaxed. Have a nice day and a successful visit. My name is Officer Hernandez, by the way,' and shook my hand! I thought 'Wow! What happened there? What a wonderful welcome to the US. What a brilliant start to the visit!'

It all goes to show how a calm mind and positive vibrations can turn a mundane and potentially stressful and unhappy situation into a joyful one, leaving all parties in a state of happiness and inner peace. It was all as a result of accepting what is! By not perceiving a situation as negative, not allowing the ego to creep into the mind to fuel anger and finding a state of inner peace, time just evaporated.

There is no room for ego when we *accept* the many things in our life that frustrate us but which we cannot change, and which are the cause of such discord, arguments and suffering. How many times do we allow ourselves to become angry and irritated by situations that are not as we would like them to be? Or by friends who do not always react the way we want them to? Do we allow our partner's little habits to frustrate us? There are all manner of things that are really quite meaningless but which our ego uses to negative effect. It is as if all the world should conform to *our* plan, whereas, in reality, we are just a small player in the Universe's much, much bigger plan.

'All the world's a stage,
And all the men and women merely players;
They have their exits and their entrances…'

—William Shakespeare, *As You Like It*

4

Eliminating Negative Thinking and Judgment

Two of the greatest barriers to finding inner peace are negative thinking and judgment.

Everything that has ever existed, that exists today and that will ever exist is the result of a thought. Every feeling or emotion that we have, every idea, every relationship, our past, our future, our beliefs, our concerns, our ambitions, our successes, our fears and hopes, they are all just our thoughts *about* these things.

Our ambitions are simply the thoughts we have generated about our future career. Our fears are just the thoughts we have about something that triggers the fear response. Other people might well react quite differently and find exciting what we think of as fearful. None of our thoughts are real. They are all illusions based on our imagination and our ego. Yet we are what we think. Our present thoughts determine our future. Our thinking decides what kind of person we want to be, the kind of life we want to lead and what matters to us.

> We are what we think. All that we are arises with our thoughts. With our thoughts we make the world.
>
> —Thomas Byrom, *The Dhammapada, the Sayings of the Buddha*

Whatever we think about expands and grows. If we think that something is possible and we have the determination to achieve it, we will always find a way. By focusing positive thoughts on what we want to achieve, we will attract what we are seeking. We will be sending out high-level positive vibrations, which will be picked up by the Universe and we will attract what we need. This is a universal law. It is immutable. We will then experience synchronicities all along the way. These appear almost as miracles yet are the Universe's natural response to high-level energetic frequencies. Everything is already here anyway.

The opposite is also true. If we hold negative beliefs, then our mind will inevitably send out low-level, heavy, negative vibrations and these will attract the same back to us. Examples of such beliefs are if we think that things cannot be achieved; we have to settle for second best; we inherited bad genes; we had a miserable childhood; we didn't have the right education; we will never be successful; our fear will always get the better of us; or fate is against us. If we start to doubt that something is possible, we also doubt ourselves and we will not achieve it. It becomes a self-fulfilling prophesy. Doubt then risks leaking into other areas of our life.

> There is nothing more dreadful than the habit of doubt. Doubt separates people. It is a poison that disintegrates friendships and breaks up pleasant relations.
>
> —Dwight Goddard, *Buddha, Truth and Brotherhood*

Negative thinking affects our mood, our attitude, our health, the aura we create, our openness and receptivity to new thinking.

It determines the kind of life we will end up living. This will be one where there is less hope, less happiness, less enthusiasm, fewer possibilities and, of course, no inner peace. Negativity destroys inner peace because our thinking is telling us that we cannot have that peace, that we are not worthy of it. The venom of negativity poisons our ability to rise above the situations we face and creates bitterness, resentment, anger and despair. If we feel unworthy, we have nothing to give that is not downhearted.

Negativity is often accompanied by judgment—another tool that ego uses to try to bolster our false sense of who we are. Judgment makes us feel superior (or inferior) and 'right", which gives us the belief that it is other people who are to blame and not ourselves.

Blaming others is handing power to others. It is allowing external factors, the behaviour of others, to determine our feelings and emotions, instead of taking responsibility for our own emotions. Others will not change because we think they should. They may not change at all. Everything that happens to us is a result of our own thinking and we cannot attribute any of it to anyone else. Blaming and judging will not solve the issues we face—it will only make them worse.

Judging others says more about us than it does about the other person. It defines us and describes our likes and dislikes. It says nothing about the other person and changes nothing. It reflects what is in *our* mind. If we judge a person negatively, then it affects all our thoughts about them. As a result, we don't like how that person looks, speaks, behaves, what they believe, how they dress, who their friends are or even what they watch on TV. These judgments are the product of our ego and will be reflected in feelings of resentment, scorn, insecurity, superiority, inferiority, envy, anger, hate and fear. These feelings have no value.

Why else do we see such enmity between people of different faiths, backgrounds, cultures and colour? These judgments are the product of our egoic mind, which makes us believe that we are right and others wrong and all that follows from that. Such negativity and judgment only perpetuate compulsive and continuous conflict, sadness, pain and suffering. It is all unnecessary. It is all mind-led and mindless. It is all the result of illusory thinking. Negativity and judgment are great barriers to achieving inner peace.

We can regain a positive attitude when we understand how our mind works. It has immense power—for good or bad. We have to understand the role our ego plays, see its destructive impact of judging others and situations negatively and how to control this. We need to realize the importance of not becoming attached to fantasies about who we think we are, to things and objects, to vanity, jealousy and neediness. We cannot completely eliminate judgment, since every thought has some judgment in it. However, you can spend time being the observer of your thoughts. Check how many times in an hour your thinking is a negative judgment, be it of a situation or a person. When others make comments, check out whether you join in or resist. Before you say anything, check what kind of judgment it is. Is it positive or negative? Think through what it might be saying about you. Remember that negative judgments are the result of negative thoughts. Negative thoughts crowd out positive ones and contaminate the mind. They will always upset your ability to find inner peace. Reduce the quantity of negative judgments and you will significantly improve the quality of your life. By reducing such judgments, you are, in effect, accepting what is. You are accepting that others have a right to be different, you are being tolerant and forgiving.

Because so much of what we read, watch and hear every day is judgmental, we live in a world that is suffering an epidemic of negative judgment. The wise will seek to avoid this in order to find their inner peace and to live on a higher spiritual plane, where what is formless reigns in unity with Oneness. Acceptance overcomes judgment and restores peace. In the Tao Te Ching, Lao Tzu explains perfectly the non-judgmental mind of the sage.

> The sage has no fixed mind;
> he is aware of the needs of others.
> Those who are good he treats with goodness.
> Those who are bad he also treats with goodness
> because the nature of his being is good.
> He is kind to the Kind.
> He is also kind to the unkind
> because the nature of his being is kindness.
> He is faithful to the faithful;
> he is also faithful to the unfaithful.
> The sage lives in harmony with all below heaven.
> He sees everything as his own self;
> he loves everyone as his own child.
> All people are drawn to him.
> He behaves like a little child.
>
> —Lao Tzu, Tao Te Ching
> (rendered by Wayne Dyer)

5

Forgiveness, Compassion, Kindness, Morality

Another barrier to inner peace we must address is when we harbour resentment or anger towards anyone we believe has harmed us or someone close to us.

We are not saying that someone who has committed unkind, hurtful, criminal or abusive acts should not be held accountable. They will have to answer for their misdeeds in the appropriate forum. But if we hold grudges, anger, hate, resentment and feelings of revenge, we join those same abusers in seeing ourselves as separate. Then we are separate from everyone else, not part of Oneness, and are acting out of ego by responding to hate with hate. We are not acting from a higher level of consciousness. Not forgiving is equivalent to making a negative judgment on a continuous basis. It is untransformed, unenlightened and not aligned to universal love. As such it is poisonous and consumes from within. It is handing power over to the perpetrator and allowing the behaviour of another to control our life.

Bearing such negative feelings is not compatible with having a spiritual existence or living a life of purpose and service.

'Father, forgive them, for they know not what they do,' are the words, according to Luke, that Jesus uttered in his agony on the cross. It is the ultimate statement of forgiveness. The most extraordinary expression of compassion and a lesson for all of us to learn and apply in our own life. Or in the words attributed to Madame de Staël, 'To understand everything is to forgive everything.' There is an enlightened, metaphysical meaning to this sentence in the link between universal understanding and love with forgiveness. One cannot exist without the other.

Forgiveness is about acceptance and giving. It is about love and kindness. If we do not have love and kindness in our soul, we will not be able to forgive others. If we cannot forgive others, we cannot forgive ourselves and if we cannot forgive ourselves, we cannot find inner peace. It is not possible to have love and only think of hate and revenge. When we are conscious of what universal love is, we awake to the importance of forgiveness as a sacred path of redemption, as in the words attributed to the Persian poet Sadi:

> The sandal-tree perfumes, when riven,
> The axe that laid it low;
> Let man who hopes to be forgiven,
> Forgive and bless his foe.

> Inner peace can be reached only when we practice forgiveness. Forgiveness is the letting go of the past and is therefore the means for correcting our misperceptions.
>
> —Gerald G Jampolsky,
> *Love Is Letting Go of Fear*

Kindness goes hand in hand with forgiveness and acceptance. Kindness is what releases tension and creates positive higher-level vibrations. It is of the spirit and in total keeping with universal love. It is about giving, has no ego, and uplifts both the one showing kindness and the receiver. Kindness promotes gentleness. St Paul considered it to be one of the nine traits of the 'fruit of the Spirit', the others being love, joy, peace, patience, goodness, faithfulness, gentleness and self-control. Kindness is one of the foundations of inner peace.

Acts of kindness should become a way of life, not an occasional event. Be kind to all those who inhabit our world, including all of nature and all fellow creatures. We protect our animals and environment, for their sakes but also for our own. We are inextricably linked.

Kindness comes in many forms, the most important factor in all cases being the desire to serve and do good. Kindness is moral and ethical and is a key agent in enlightenment and awakening to universal intelligence.

> The highest virtue is to act without a sense of self.
> The highest kindness is to give without condition.
> The highest justice is to see without preference.
>
> —Lao Tzu, Tao Te Ching
> (rendered by Wayne Dyer)

6

Gratitude, Awe, Joy, Enthusiasm, Appreciation

Inner peace is also achieved when we have a sense of awe about the world, about nature, about man's positive achievements and infinite capacity. We should take time to wonder at the beauty all around us: the creative capabilities of human beings but also of nature, flowers, insects, birds, animals, the sea, the sky, the galaxies, which act out miraculous feats in front of our eyes every day. Ego has no space to exist in this wondrous environment. We are free to simply look in amazement. We do not need to label or intellectualize. We can simply *be* and *feel* their sacred presence, their connection to the universal consciousness, peace and love to which we all belong.

This awe provides us with an enthusiasm for life and for our everyday actions, for our relationships, our family, our work and our play. Enthusiasm, which means 'possessed by a god' or 'in God', has a high-energy frequency, and, being entirely egoless, sends positive and light vibrations into the Universe. It affects all within its reach with contagious optimism. Enthusiasm needs nothing because it has everything it requires. Enthusiasm is the fuel of achievement and is the ultimate expression of being in the moment.

In this space, there are no concerns about past or fears about future, only an electric current or force field that brings us closer to the energy field of our conscious essence. Undertaking everything that we do with enthusiasm is the best way of eliminating stress and finding inner peace. It is the best way of turning any ordeal into a divine adventure.

This is the tale of the two quarrymen. They were hewing large rocks into smaller square blocks. It was back-breaking physical work, paid fairly poorly and with little scope for recognition or advancement. Asked what they were doing, the first said he was hacking into the rock face in order to make appropriately sized blocks. The second, when asked the same question, said: 'I am helping to build a cathedral. It will be the most beautiful place of worship in our city and thousands will come to pray there every day, including my children and their children after them. My work needs to be of the highest precision to meet the expectation we have of this sacred building. I cannot express what a privilege and a joy it is to be associated with such a project.'

As we focus just on the moment itself, when we are fully present and feel the aliveness of our being, we enter into a state of joy. This is where the zest for life and a healthy sense of fun resides. This joy connects us to the infinite power of the Universe, the power of all creation, with which it resonates completely. We are in the moment—the only place where life can be truly lived and from which we can be transported to a higher plane. This is conscious awareness and the link between our transient, mortal existence and our divine, eternal soul. Here we become consciously aware that we are truly alive and free.

At this point, we experience a deep sense of gratitude for the many wonderful and beautiful things in our human life. Gratitude implies humility—a recognition that we are blessed by the goodness that comes from others and from the Universe. Gratitude and ego cannot co-exist, because gratitude gives no room for resentment, fear or conflict. It is not about self-aggrandizement or false images of self. Gratitude is not about wanting or needing anything, since it has everything it needs already. In many ways, it is inner peace itself.

7

Stillness, Self and Purpose

Inner peace is stillness. Stillness is silence. Silence is divine.

> God's one and only voice is silence.
>
> —Herman Melville

Nature is silent and the trees, the flowers, the plants, the constellations, the sun, the moon, the planets are silent. They grow and move in silence.

> Silence of the heart is necessary so you can hear God everywhere—in the closing of a door, in the person who needs you, in the birds that sing, in the flowers, in the animals.
>
> —Mother Teresa

Silence is no-sound. Space is emptiness. Emptiness is no-space. Silence and space are formless. They cannot be touched, heard, grasped, tasted or smelled; only intuitively and spiritually perceived. Yet we know they exist and are fundamental to existence. Without silence there can be no sound. Without space there can be no objects. Music can only be heard because of the silence between the notes. A room can only exist because of the space contained between the walls. A glass is only of use because of the void in its centre. A wheel can only be used because of the empty hub holding the spokes.

> The usefulness of what is
> depends on what is not.
>
> —Lao Tzu, Tao Te Ching

Inner peace depends on stillness and silence, on what cannot be measured or seen but is fundamental to consciousness, to spiritual awakening and universal love.

> All of humanity's problems stem from man's inability to sit quietly in a room alone.
>
> —Blaise Pascal

Why do we find it so hard to sit still, quietly and alone for any length of time without looking for some form of distraction? Because, when forced to sit still and silently, we are faced with the unending stream of chatter from our ego—mainly about how difficult mortal life is—and we would rather avoid this. Gillian Anderson reflects the thoughts of many when she says, 'I have a real problem with stillness. With just stopping and being quiet.'

We fill the space with fidgeting, looking for our mobile, sending texts, playing games and generally finding things to distract our mind—anything to evade the silence. Yet this is the very occasion when we have an opportunity to confront and defeat our ego. Ego is not comfortable with silence because if we learn to sit in silence and reflect deeply and calmly, we will confront it. More importantly, in that silence, we go beyond our ego to the discovery of who we are, where we came from and where we are going. We find our true self. We find that life is much more than the ego portrays it.

Finding the peace of stillness and silence heralds the end of ego. Rediscovering who we are and the power to lead a life free of ego brings a sense of peace and contentment that no temporary pleasure created by ego can possibly emulate. Inner peace can only be found in silence, in stillness and in the *now*. Far from being a place to fear, as so many of us do, silence is a place of truth, healing and peace.

> In the stillness of your presence, you can feel your own formless and timeless reality as the unmanifested life that animates your physical form.... You look beyond the veil of form and separation. This is the realization of Oneness.
>
> —Eckhart Tolle

The practice of meditation enables this stillness and silence to be experienced. It takes time but it works and is a prime source of finding peace. It is a form of prayer. However, rather than speaking to God, you connect to higher intelligence and listen to what the Universe is saying. You feel a divine presence of which we are also a part. It is not an intellectual exercise and cannot be comprehended by reasoning and rationality. It can only be experienced and felt. Meditation and ego cannot co-exist because one is focused on presence and being in the now, while the other is about conflict, past time, future time and a false sense of self.

Who are we anyway? Who are you? Who am I?

We have already established what we are not. We are not our name. That is simply what our parents decided to call us. We are not our title, occupation, the image we have of ourselves, the image others have of us, what we have or what we do. Our occupation is what we do, not who we are. If we were our image or what we did, when we stopped doing those things or being that image, we would cease to exist, which is clearly not the case. And we are not our possessions—however much we sometimes use them as a means of defining us—they are just things. Nor are we our thoughts either. They are, of course, the product of our mind, but they are not who we are, since, with a little effort, we can become the observers of our thoughts. If we are the observers of our thoughts, we cannot be those thoughts at the same time.

Being an observer means that we are creating a distance, a space between who we are and our thoughts. Awakening to the separation between thought and being, between form and formless is the beginning of conscious awareness.

Conscious awareness is a recognition that all the thoughts that we have are the product of our human condition with its ego, conditioned memories, needs and wants, whereas who we truly are is the observer of them. We are the presence that is able to see the thoughts and experience the emotions as they are being created. This observer is detached from our everyday trials and tribulations and sees things in perspective. This is the I AM, the undefinable essence of our spiritual presence, our conscious awareness. When Moses asked, 'Who shall I say you are?' to the voice that spoke to him from the burning bush, the answer was 'I am that I am'—divine, undefinable, infinite, eternal, formless.

Who we are, our conscious awareness, is part of the conscious awareness of the Universe itself. We *are* conscious awareness. We are connected to universal intelligence and infinite love in this energetic, all-encompassing matrix. We are one and the same. Our true presence has a depth that is infinitely deeper than that of our mortal body. While our life has a horizontal dimension (since all our activities take place sequentially and in a linear fashion) our soul has a deep vertical dimension and is timeless.

Imagine an ocean. Our life is what happens on the surface, with its storms, waves, calm periods, even shipwrecks. Who we *are* is the ocean itself—in all its depth and mystery. We are the giant canvas on which various scenes are painted and repainted. We are the conscious dreamer in our own dream. We are capable of altering the course of our life, since, being detached observers, we have power over our thoughts, rather than they having power over us. We have the capacity to do almost anything.

> 'For truly, I say to you, if you have faith like a grain of mustard seed, you will say to this mountain, "Move from here to there," and it will move, and nothing will be impossible for you.'
>
> —Matthew 17:20

Understanding who we are is enormously empowering as well as a source of great relief. We are no longer the servant of our needs and wants, our resentments and anger about the past or our fears about the future. We are no longer jostled in every direction by the randomness of events, which are ultimately meaningless. Stress ceases to exist when we awaken to the realization that our mortal existence is separate from our spiritual being and that we can disassociate ourselves from ego and, hence, from conflict, pain and suffering. In discovering who we are, we have discovered inner peace.

We still need to make plans and undertake all the activities of our mortal life while we live it. We cannot live with our heads in the clouds or oblivious to the requirements of the everyday. The point, however, is that we can approach everything we do without judgment, without trying to control everything. We have a better perspective and balance and a sense of calm. What we then 'do' comes from a good place—a place of peace, kindness, forgiveness, awe, enthusiasm and joy.

What should we do then? What should be our purpose?

Our main purpose should be to ensure that we live our life in alignment with universal intelligence and truth. This means: being consciously aware of our thoughts; practising the art of remaining detached from them; accepting what we cannot change or control; not wanting to be 'right' all the time; living in the present moment; surrendering to what is; being humble, grateful, compassionate and kind; and behaving according to these practices.

This may seem like a huge list of impossible and utopic, even saintly, requirements. In reality, it is only returning to the state of normality and purity that existed before our conditioned ego took over. It does not mean we cannot operate in the 'real' world or say no to what is not appropriate. On the contrary, it gives us the strength to know that when things are wrong, we know how to act from a place of wisdom. It enables us to truly love unconditionally. It enables us to see that all 'things' are transient and cannot be taken with us, so can be enjoyed for what they are.

Being aligned with universal love means that whatever we choose to do, whatever our plans and projects—and we all have something special to contribute—we will do them from a place of goodness and not because of the dictates of our ego. We will reflect the guiding principles of the Universe. We brought nothing into this world and we will take nothing out. All we have to give is our life and what is in our heart. It is up to us that what we have to give is the most positive it can possibly be.

Our purpose for 'doing' will be service to others. It will be about giving, helping, supporting, teaching, healing. We will accept, observe, enable and encourage with wisdom, enthusiasm, humility and passion. We will act in a spirit of pure love with no expectation, no demands, no sense of entitlement.

> Everything under heaven is a sacred vessel and cannot
> be controlled.
> Trying to control leads to ruin.
> Trying to grasp, we lose.
> Allow your life to unfold naturally.
> Know that it too is a vessel of perfection....
> To the sage all of life is a movement toward perfection,
> so what need has he for the excessive, the extravagant or
> the extreme?
>
> —Lao Tzu, Tao Te Ching
> (rendered by Wayne Dyer)

8

Living a New Way of Life

Peace comes from within. Do not seek it without.

—Anonymous

As human beings, we live at a time when we have discovered the capacity to exterminate all life in many different ways and with greater and greater ease. There is a tremendous need, then, for the human race to change the way it thinks in order to change the way it lives and, ultimately, change the world we live in.

The fear that dominates our life, which is the product of our individual and collective ego, has created a world of anxiety, lies, false truths, fake news and illusion. It has also put our world in extreme danger. The news reports, the conflicts and seemingly unending stream of dark information only serve to invade our minds with negativity—a negativity that spawns more negativity. The result is division and separateness, the re-emergence of nationalism, which is divisive, the worsening of knife crime, suicide rates, depression and anxiety.

In a study carried out in 2015, more than a quarter of US workers reported some level of depression or anxiety. Worldwide, some 700 million people suffer from mental health issues. Meanwhile, the number of wild animals has reduced by sixty percent since 1970. The threat from biological pathogens has increased dramatically. Global warming is now a very well-known issue with massive implications and we have enough nuclear bombs to destroy the world many times over. Information technology and the ability to manipulate and use data in every conceivable way can be beneficial but it is also one of the greatest perils facing us, since it pervades every aspect of life and can exacerbate every issue raised in this paragraph.

Concentrating on these negative risks, however, will not provide the answer to our problems. Science is neutral. It can be used for good as well as bad. Information technology is neutral. Both of these just *are*. They have no point of view. They used to simply do what they were asked to do. Increasingly, they may also be self-programming and do what they 'want' to do, without recourse to human intervention. The last financial crisis was certainly made worse by the stampede of automatic responses of computer algorithms setting off a domino series of instructions to sell.

The only answer is for the human race to realize that a new way of thinking is required. With this will come new institutions, new charters, new protocols but, above all, a new understanding of the catastrophic and inevitable risks of not doing anything and expecting improvement. Without action to change, no improvements will be forthcoming, and the world will continue down its road to extinction. Earth will survive. It has many years in which to recover. But humankind will disappear along with all the species that animate this beautiful world.

And it will all have been utterly senseless. Astronauts who have set foot on the moon or in space have wondered in awe at the immense beauty, fragility and infinitely tiny nature of this amazing planet.

> I thought at one point, if you could be up in heaven, this is how you would see the planet. And then I dwelled on that and said no, it's more beautiful than that. This is what heaven must look like. I think of our planet as a paradise. We are lucky to be here.
>
> —Mike Massimino, NASA astronaut

> It suddenly struck me that that tiny pea, pretty and blue, was the earth. I put up my thumb and shut one eye, and my thumb blotted out the planet Earth. I didn't feel like a giant. I felt very, very small.
>
> —Neil Armstrong, NASA astronaut and first man on the moon

It is possible to change the way we think, individually and collectively, if we choose a different path: one of inner peace and not conflict. Across the world and across all age groups, genders, colours and creeds, many, many people believe this change is necessary and timely. One has only to look at the reactions of people across the world to the horrors of war, malnutrition, child poverty and homelessness, all types of pollution, as well as race, disability and gender discrimination to realize the groundswell of collective opinion in favour of addressing and eliminating these dangers.

It can happen as it has happened before with such issues as slavery, universal suffrage, independence and civil rights. All it takes is enough people collectively with enough will to want to make change happen for it to happen. All it takes is for people to say, 'Enough is enough.' They can force changes in leadership and insist that leaders act for the benefit of mankind and not out of selfish, greedy or egoistic motives. The checks and balances that are so important to stable and safe government need to be upheld and enhanced.

It is up to us now and we must give the world the best we have. Nothing else will do.

1. People are illogical, unreasonable, and self-centred. Love them anyway.
2. If you do good, people will accuse you of selfish ulterior-motives. Do good anyway.
3. If you are successful, you win false friends and true enemies. Succeed anyway.
4. The good you do today will be forgotten tomorrow. Do good anyway.
5. Honesty and frankness make you vulnerable. Be honest and frank anyway.
6. The biggest men with the biggest ideas can be shot down by the smallest men with the smallest minds. Think big anyway.
7. People favour underdogs but follow only top dogs. Fight for a few underdogs anyway.
8. What you spend years building may be destroyed overnight. Build anyway.

9. People really need help but may attack you if you do help them. Help people anyway.
10. Give the world the best you have and you'll get kicked in the teeth. Give the world the best you have anyway.

—Kent M. Keith, 'Paradoxical Commandments of Leadership'

PART 2

The Laws *of the* Universe

When We Awaken

We only realize it was all just a dream,
When we awaken
The laughs and the tears
The worries and fears
The heat of the race
The thrill of the chase
The random encounters, the crazy delights
The joyful reunions, the meaningless fights
It all seemed so real, such colour, such life
The sounds so acute, as sharp as a knife
No cause, no effect, no logic, no sense
Unconscious thoughts, some vivid, some dense
We only realize it was all just *a* dream
When we awaken
The stress and the strain
The hurt and the pain
The conflict and suffering
The wars all destroying
The glitz and the glamour
The champagne and clamour
The greed and the wealth
The destruction of health
The obsession with fame, with image, with body

What man calls his triumph and God calls his folly
It doesn't exist, it's all an illusion
Mind's thoughts a delusion, constructed confusion
An absence of soul, a belief in mere 'things'
Courting disaster, the danger bell rings
We only realize it was all just *our* dream
When we awaken
Through darkness and night
To fight for what's right
Compassion and hope, forgiveness, acceptance
No expectation, no debt, no inner resistance
A passion for honesty, authenticity, connection
To beauty, to nature, to holy reflection
Pure Joy, sacred spirit, mankind's Inner Peace,
Unconditional love, the final release
Till at last we perceive the ultimate truth
Heaven's here, right now;
Within you, within me
Conscious awareness, Eternal Light; it can be... let it be
We only realize it is all just *God's* dream
When we awaken

—Vernon Sankey

9

Oneness—the All Is Mind

Have you ever felt completely at peace with yourself and the world? Maybe while sitting looking at a beautiful sunset or at the waves lapping the beach?

Have you ever felt totally relaxed, happy and contented in the company of your family or close friends?

Have you ever felt an inner sense of joy because you defused a potentially angry exchange or made an unhappy person happy?

Have you ever been so in the moment, so emotionally engaged, that your whole being became imbued with a beautiful feeling of complete wellbeing?

Have you ever experienced an intense feeling of warmth, of love and of the divine nature of the Universe?

Have you ever felt so authentic and true and in harmony with yourself that you were enveloped in a glow of happiness?

If you have ever experienced any feelings and emotions such as these, you have experienced the beauty of Oneness.

Oneness occurs when the different parts of our being, of our body and our soul, unite together harmoniously, as ONE. We then feel whole and at peace with ourselves.

In this state, there is no place for the anxious, fearful, resentful or stressful thoughts that tend to dominate our everyday thinking, however trivial these thoughts often are.

We cannot be whole if, in our busy life, we are so angry about the past or so fearful about what may or may not happen tomorrow that we have no time to enjoy the simplicity and beauty of the present moment, the NOW.

Negative thoughts assault us and create a separation of the soul from the body, which results in a painful and an uncomfortable tension. We feel there is something missing and we feel unhappy.

Inner peace, harmony and happiness can only be achieved when these anxieties and tensions are eliminated, and we return to a state of Oneness.

Why is this the case? What is happening here?

Oneness is a recognition that we are all a tiny microcosm of one large macrocosm—the Universe. We all came from one source and we will all return to that same source; however we choose to describe it.

Some will describe the eternal, unchanging and unchangeable source as God (or by whatever name they give God). Some will describe it as the eternal light, the All, the One, the universal, infinite, living Mind, the truth or the Word. Scientists describe it as energy. Ultimately, it is the love of God that 'passes all understanding'.

Most religions and spiritual beliefs, ways or paths refer to this Eternal Source in one way or another, as these quotations from Christianity, Hermeticism, Sikhism and Islam show:

> In the beginning was the Word. And the Word was with God. And the Word was God!
>
> —John 1:1

'I am that Light ... the idea of beautiful order, the harmony of all things with all things.... Life is the union of Mind and Word.... Fix your attention upon the Light and become One with it.'

—*Corpus Hermeticum*

The ALL is MIND; the Universe is Mental.

—*The Kybalion*

There is but one all-pervading spirit, and It is called the Truth, It exists in all creation, and It has no fear, It does not hate and It is timeless, universal and self-existent!

—Sri Guru Granth Sahib

He is God, who is One. God, the Eternal Refuge. He neither begets nor is born. Nor is there to him any equivalent.

—Quran, 112:1–4

All of these interpretations are 'right' since they are all referring to the same mystical and marvellous phenomenon—a higher plain of energy, a heaven—that defines our very existence and from which we receive inspiration, intuition and guidance.

Prayer is when we talk to the Divine, intuition is when the Divine replies.

Because we are all particles of energy emanating from that same single source, we are all part of that same Oneness. We are all connected, interconnected and interdependent. We are, in effect, all part of the same family. The actions of any one family member will be felt by and have repercussions on all the others. This applies to all aspects of our world and all the creatures that live on it since they too are part of the same Oneness.

We came from the same source and we will all return to it when our physical body dies.

All the thoughts and actions we have automatically affect everything else—whether we like it or not and even whether we are aware of their impact or not.

> Whatever is below, is like that which is above; and that which is above, is like that which is below. By this are acquired and perfected the Miracles of the One Thing.
>
> —Hermes Trismegistus,
> *The Emerald Tablet*

What is meant by this quotation is that everything that exists—whether in heaven (above) or earth (below)—is encompassed in the One and cannot be disassociated. The Universe was created by the One (commonly called God). The recognition that what is above (divine and heavenly) affects and is part of what is below (earthly, matter) and what is below affects and can become what is above, constitutes the 'Miracle of the One Thing'.

Whatever happens anywhere, and on any level, whether physical, mental, spiritual or emotional, happens on every other level.

> Though we are many, we are one body.
>
> —The Book of Common Prayer

To think there is any possibility of acting in splendid isolation with no effect on anything else is pointless. We cannot.

Even if we think we can do something in total secrecy, unknown to anyone else, without impact, we cannot. Whatever we do will affect our own body and mind and have an effect on our own thinking and our behaviour, which will then, inevitably, affect others and the harmonious state of the All. We are what we think. Our very thinking will have created thought waves or vibrations that cause extensive ripples.

We rarely recognize—let alone take the time to examine why we feel so deeply uncomfortable and unhappy—when we are not 'at one' with ourselves. We tend to assume others are to blame or we have suffered 'bad luck'. We do not realize that blaming others only produces yet more negative effects and that 'chance' or 'fate' is always the result of some cause outside of ourselves, even if we do not understand what that cause is. 'Chance' is never a purely random occurrence.

Oneness implies we have an immortal soul and a transient body. We have a unique opportunity to use this divine gift of life to do good things for the world, in love and compassion, thereby keeping our soul and body together as One.

The love affair many have with the body and the obsession with the material (and the attendant ego-driven need to own, control and dominate) have led us to forget about our soul, our inner Being and our spirituality. It is only through nurturing our spirituality that we can acquire wisdom, compassion and love.

All the anger, resentment and conflicts are the result of thinking egotistically, thinking we are *separate* rather than part of the same Oneness. By thinking we are separate, we start to look for differences instead of similarities. We also start to think that our 'separateness' must be the result of our superior knowledge, belief system or even race.

We then internalize these thoughts and when they are questioned, we become defensive.

Many wars have been fought because one group felt they were 'separate', different, better than another. Our religion is right and yours is wrong! My interpretation of events is the truth, so yours must be a lie. We are the 'master race' and must purge the world of 'undesirables'! We fight and destroy each other based on thoughts that are not only intrinsically evil but entirely insane. These thoughts are founded on a complete lack of understanding of the universal importance of Oneness.

If we are truly One, what is the point of fighting ourselves? It makes no sense.

Because we are ignorant of the vital importance of being whole, we just drift on—often in intense anxiety and pain—powerless to remedy our situation. We are ignorant of how to take responsibility for our own future, let alone help others to do so.

The result is that we have created an illusory world, which has become selfish, cruel and dangerous. In this world, the superficial and trivial, instant gratification and mindless activity assume greater and greater importance at the expense of gaining wisdom and understanding, acceptance and peace. We are obsessed by things and images. These obsessions turn out, sooner or later, to be just illusions. They are not real, yet they are often believed to be real. This causes great suffering and stress as we try to imitate or live up to images and ideas that are completely false.

Is it any surprise that so many people are lost and in despair, so many children are depressed and the suicide rate is so high? Is it any surprise that so many are in desperate need of comfort, compassion and help? People are suffering deeply because of beliefs and expectations that are delusions. These delusions give priority to unstable, temporary and ultimately unreal objects and images, at the expense of the mind, beauty, truth, love, understanding and wisdom.

We need to regain and nurture wisdom in order to help resolve the world's truly important (and potentially apocalyptic) problems and return to a state of Oneness. We need to evolve our thinking and understand the importance of Oneness.

> Einstein said an interesting thing, 'The world that we have made as a result of the level of thinking we have done thus far creates problems that we cannot solve at the same level as the level we created them at.'
>
> —Ram Dass

What this makes clear is that we need to evolve our *thinking* to a new, higher level if we are to resolve the increasingly complex problems that we have created here on earth. Why would understanding Oneness be so important in helping us to achieve this?

Oneness means that the One, God or Eternal Light (or however one wishes to describe the Creator) made the Universe. The Universe was the product of a *thought* that emanated from this universal power. Everything that exists and has ever existed is a thought from this power. Or as the *Kybalion* puts it: 'All is Mind.' It is the Mind that has created the Oneness and the Mind that provides harmony and unity.

As human beings we have an immensely powerful mind. Our mind is, by implication, modelled on the Mind of the One, since we are part of the One.

Everything that we see, feel, think and experience—whether it be 'real' or 'unreal'—sits inside our mind. Everything that exists *and has ever existed* is a thought within this amazing and unique instrument we call our mind.

> All that we are is a result of what we have thought.
>
> —The Dhammapada

Our mind encompasses everything. We can picture what we had for breakfast this morning, where we went on holiday last year, who we're seeing tomorrow, what we need to buy in the supermarket, how we felt when we lost the game with the children, how we are feeling reading this book, all instantly through one thing: our mind.

Our mind is our "oneness" in that it brings together all our experiences. It also brings together all the opposites and contradictions, all positive and negative thoughts, all joys and all sadness. We cannot experience these at the same time with our body, but we can with our mind. And in this quality, our mind mirrors the Oneness of God's Mind, which unites all of the Universe and everything that may have gone before or will happen after.

We thus have an opportunity and a responsibility. By applying the power of our own mind and modelling it to the Mind of the One, we can search for and find new and better ways to address the problems of our world.

Given our understanding of Oneness, here are some important questions for us to consider:

- Would we willingly cause harm to anyone else if we knew they were part of our own family?

- Would we seek to accumulate so many material things if we realized that our gratification might leave other family members without?
- Would we seek to accumulate so much if there was no one else around to impress or to admire us?
- Would we condone—by our silence—or endorse violence on our close relatives?
- Would we stand by and do nothing if we were aware that our own sons and daughters were so hounded by internet bullying that they sought solace in suicide?

The anger and frustration we have for others is the anger and frustration we have towards ourselves. When we criticize 'other people', we are actually only talking about ourselves. When we harm others, we harm ourselves. 'We' and 'they' are all part of that same One.

We cannot love others if we cannot love ourselves since they are part of us and we are part of them. If we cannot love others, we can never enjoy inner peace and harmony or the joy of spiritual Oneness.

> Searching all directions with one's awareness, one finds no
> one dearer
> than oneself.
> In the same way, others are dear to themselves.
> So one should not hurt others if one loves oneself.
>
> —The Udana

To love the self requires an internal, not an external, focus. It requires us to be mindful of who we are and our thoughts. It requires us to learn to be in continuous connection with our true essence, our soul, our own unique Oneness.

Unconditional love is the divine quality of our intrinsic nature. It is not the result of some intellectual abstract thought process. We have to experience and feel it deeply and internally.

> The Buddha [said], 'It is like when someone points his finger at the moon to show it to someone else. Guided by the finger, that person should see the moon. If he looks at the finger instead and mistakes it for the moon, he loses not only the moon but the finger also.'
>
> —The Shurangama

The impact of negative, ego-driven actions on our individual and collective conscience forces a separation of our soul from our body and prevents us from returning to that Oneness we so assuredly need to attain. In this state of separation, we cannot find peace. Yet that is what we are constantly doing—every day of every year. Sometimes individually, sometimes with others, we think and act in a collective ignorance. We are carried on a wave of misunderstanding and misinformation that leads to actual and potentially catastrophic consequences, affecting billions of fellow creatures.

Although every day across our world, there are many wonderful examples of kindness, unselfishness and love, we should be ashamed at the enormity of the distortions, greed and ego-driven acts of self-destruction that dominate our landscape and pollute our lives and our world. The ultimate irony (and an example of the destructive power of our obsession with the body and our egos) is the fact there is enough food and abundance on earth today to enable all of our

7.6 billion co-habitants to live a decent life—with enough to eat, a roof over their heads, proper education and in peace.

Instead, we have over 3 billion living in poverty, 1.3 billion live in extreme poverty and nearly 1 billion are hungry. And approximately, 22,000 children die each day due to poverty. Across the world, 70 million people are displaced. In the last century, more than 100 million people were killed in wars. All of this is man-made—the result of the actions of so-called human beings. All of this is avoidable. All of this could be different. All of this could be changed. All of these divisions could be reconciled to bring the world back to Oneness.

Whenever, by our thoughts and actions, we divide the One into two, harmony cannot exist. Harmony is at the opposite pole to the egoic sense of self that causes us to feel separate and different. The egoic sense is the cause of so much conflict and prevents us from being One with Life. For harmony to exist, we must be One with Life.

> There are three words that convey the secret of the art of living, the secret of all success and happiness: One with Life. Being One with life is being One with Now. You then realize that you don't live your life, but life lives you. Life is the dancer, and you are the dance.
>
> —Eckhart Tolle

The principle of Oneness makes clear that we are all part of one Universe and from one source. Therefore, since our thoughts and actions inevitably affect everything else, we should first examine our own mind.

We need to understand who we really are and how we have become that person. 'As I think, I am.' Thinking is where it all begins. The 'Mind' as well as the heart lie at the centre of this process.

> The ALL is MIND … The ALL is but ONE.
>
> —*The Kybalion*

Our present thoughts determine our future. Taking time to examine our thoughts and where they come from is essential in order to understand why we act, react and do the things we do. Our destiny is determined, not by what happens to us, but how we react and respond. Our response will be the product of our thoughts and the quality of those thoughts.

> The aphorism, "as a man thinketh in his heart so is he" not only embraces the whole of man's being but is so comprehensive as to reach out to every condition and circumstance of his life. A man is literally *what he thinks,* his character being the complete sum of all his thoughts.
>
> —James Allen, *As a Man Thinketh*

Our minds and thoughts are the product of our past and the way we look at the world is the result of everything that we have already experienced in our life. Where did these ideas come from? Who put them in our head? Did whoever put them there really know? Are our ideas and beliefs based on truths or someone else's perception of the truth?

Whether true or false, our beliefs have all been acquired from the past: from our parents, teachers and friends; from what we read and heard; from what we have experienced. In consequence, we have developed our attitudes to life—positive or negative, prejudiced or liberal, reflective or instinctive, harsh or gentle.

However, are these beliefs helpful to us? Are they based on truth, kindness and compassion? Taking time to understand how our own mind thinks and why we react the way we do to different stimuli is an important start. Examining critically the basis for our thoughts and reactions—rather than blindly accepting those thoughts as inevitable truths—is equally important.

Socrates articulated one of the key messages of the principle of Oneness when he said, 'An unexamined life is not worth living.'

The principle of Oneness asks us to think very carefully before we do anything, as each thought and action affects everything else. It asks us to go even beyond this and become the observer of our thoughts by creating space for objectivity and balance.

When we are faced with a challenge, we can react in one of two ways: If we react by thinking negative thoughts, we will create negative intentions and that is what we will receive in return. If we react with positive thoughts, then that is what we will receive in return. The consequence of any challenge is decided by the thinking behind our response. It is always up to us to take responsibility for our reaction and its consequences.

> Every thought-seed sown or allowed to fall into the mind, and to take root there, produces its own, blossoming sooner or later into act, and bearing its own fruitage of opportunity and circumstance. Good thoughts bear good fruit, bad thoughts bad fruit.
>
> —James Allen, *As a Man Thinketh*

Many well-intentioned people project negativity because they harbour anger about their assumed powerlessness over the past and the present. They then transmit negative 'vibrations', which become self-fulfilling because they see many more negatives than positives in situations. As the proverb says, we reap what we sow. As a consequence, people become victims and not victors of circumstances. Blaming, accusing, assuming the worst becomes an alternative to taking responsibility. The cause of seemingly negative events is often ascribed to past experiences and events. Certainly, the past may cast huge shadows on the present, but this should not be used as an excuse for negativity or a crutch for inactivity and passivity.

Before we do anything, we should consider the following question: Is what I am thinking right now (and hence likely to act on) based on a negative or ego-driven approach and the product of past frustration, resentment or anger, or is it positive and based on compassion, understanding and love?

If the former, then before you do anything, stop! Change your thinking from negative to positive, from hate to love. Have the courage to surmount your acquired instinct for looking at the world in a negative way. How can you do this? By using your *imagination* to create a *positive image* in your mind and substituting that for the negative one. It takes a bit of effort, but it is not difficult. With practice, it becomes second nature.

By consciously using our powerful mind and imagination to create new, better images on a regular basis for small things, we come to realize we can also do the same for bigger things. The solutions all lie in our own mind—for which we need to take full responsibility. Only then will we be able to address the biggest issues we and the world face.

As the scientist Lothar Schäfer writes: 'I define mind as the realm of inner images in us that guide our life. In our mind, these images find a special level of reality in our consciousness. The concept of the "inner images" ... guides and steers the reactions and actions of living beings.'

It is these images that we create and store that give meaning to our life and predetermine how we act. Being mindful of them by taking time to think and mastering them by changing them are, therefore, essential steps to transforming a negative mindset into a positive one and moving from separation and disunity to Oneness.

Here is another question to ask yourself: Are my thoughts and actions based on personal responsibility for my role in the universe or are they the result of an kneejerk reaction to defend myself against 'attacks' on my ego and the 'slights' of the past?

If the latter, then stop! Consider the role your ego is playing here. Is it helping or hindering you? Is it stopping you taking a good decision because of its need to be 'right'? Change your defensive thoughts by creating a positive image of yourself doing the right thing and keep it in your mind. Concentrate on your opportunity to be responsible and caring.

Similarly, consider if your thoughts and actions are governed by the need to win, control and prop up your self-esteem? Or, conversely, are they based on understanding, patience, kindness and the desire to protect, nurture and love?

It is very valuable to spend time on these questions. We should continuously test our thoughts, actions and reactions against the idea of Oneness on a systematic basis, so as to create a new habit of thinking before acting.

The results will be highly beneficial.

If we take a little time to consciously think and act out of love and compassion and override any negative self-talk from our subconscious mind, we will inevitably behave in a healthier, more responsible and kinder way. Our masculine and feminine sides will be more in balance—as will our whole being. We will transmit higher vibrations that will resonate widely, bringing us and the universe to a better place.

The small gestures are as important as the large ones: just smiling rather than walking past; helping rather than ignoring; acknowledging rather than dismissing; accepting rather than disputing; letting go rather than struggling futilely; surrendering rather than fighting; being authentic rather than devious. All these positive attributes help to restore equilibrium between the body and the soul and bring us back to Oneness and unconditional love.

> In the stillness of your presence, you can feel your own formless and timeless reality as the unmanifested life that animates your physical form. You can then feel the same life deep within every other human and every other creature. You look beyond the veil of form and separation. This is the realization of Oneness. This is love. What is God? The eternal One Life underneath all the forms of life. What is Love? To feel the presence of that One Life deep within yourself and within all creatures. To be it. Therefore all love is the love of God.
>
> —Eckhart Tolle, *The Power of Now*

A final thought to conclude this chapter on the principle of Oneness: We have a choice. We always have a choice. If we have the will, courage and desire to solve the problems that face us—as individuals and the world—we will find we have the key to solving them. It is up to us to take responsibility. We need to take the power that we have and not to give it to others who will use it for their own purposes. Our beautiful world, our beautiful universe, our beautiful children deserve no less.

> For man is separated into soul and body, and only when the two sides of his sense agree together, does utterance of its thoughts conceived by mind take place.
>
> For it is mind that doth conceive all thoughts—good thoughts when it receives the seeds from God, the opposite when received from Evil.
>
> —*Corpus Hermeticum*

Consider this little story. While sitting in a cemetery one day, contemplating God and the Universe, a young woman, Katey, was writing some pages of her book. A little girl appeared with her father. She turned, and for no particular reason, other than she felt comfortable that another gentle soul was around, she asked the young woman, 'Where does God live?' The woman thought for a moment and looked into the pure, innocent eyes of the child. It was a beautiful, wonderful, magical moment. The little girl's father looked perplexed, not knowing how to answer such an apparently difficult question. The young woman then said, 'God is in you.' The little girl looked down at her body and replied, 'But, where is he? I can't see him!' The young woman replied, 'No, it's not a person who you can see with your eyes or someone who lives in the clouds. It is the love you have in your heart.' The little girl looked at her father and he looked at her and they hugged each other with an immense feeling of love, grateful to have shared such a beautiful moment.

In the words attributed to Carl Jung: Your vision will become clear when you can look into your own heart. Who looks outside, dreams; who looks inside, awakes.

> I sent my Soul through the Invisible,
> Some letter of that After-life to spell:
> And by and by my Soul return'd to me,
> And answer'd 'I Myself am Heav'n and Hell.'
>
> —Omar Khayyam, *Rubaiyat,* LXVI,
> translated by Edward FitzGerald

> In our modern society everything seems geared to material development, even our systems of education. As a result, we no longer pay sufficient attention to our inner values, which leads to mental unrest. In order to address this imbalance, we need to pay more attention to our minds.
>
> —Dalai Lama

10

Everything Is Energy and Everything Vibrates

Have you ever wondered why some people seem to be consistently upbeat and happy, exuding a certain *joie de vivre,* and others seem to be anchored to negative thoughts and always miserable?

Have you observed how for some the glass is 'half full' while for others it is 'half empty'?

Have you ever noticed how some people seem to always have 'bad luck' in spite of making real efforts to succeed, while others seem to sail through with 'luck' on their side and apparently not a care in the world?

Have you observed how some people are always in the company of fun, happy, easy-going people, who laugh and enjoy life, while others seem to be surrounded by more grumpy, cynical, unhappy, complaining people?

The Kybalion, a book that examines the Hermetic philosophy of Ancient Egypt and Greece, says, 'Nothing rests; everything moves; everything vibrates.'

> Everything is energy. Match the frequency of the reality you want, and you cannot help but get that reality. It can be no other way. This is not philosophy. This is physics.
>
> —Darryl Anka

Everything in the universe is energy. All that we see around us, including ourselves, is moving, vibrating and travelling in a circular pattern at a specific frequency. This includes, most importantly, our own thoughts and attitudes. These we send out, wittingly or unwittingly, into the Universe. Their specific frequency is picked up by those operating on a similar 'wavelength'.

Modern-day quantum physics has shown us that at the sub-atomic level everything is energy, and everything has its own vibrational frequency. This allows us to see and distinguish that which is physically separate from us. This is how we recognize that this form is another person or a flower or a dog.

By detecting quanta, or the tiniest particles measurable, we find that any 'matter', such as a piece of paper or a pencil, consists ultimately of only empty space and energy that is constantly vibrating. Thus, everything that appears solid is, in fact, the vibration of the energy that makes it up. The denser the object, the higher the speed of vibration and the lower the density, the lower the speed of vibration.

Science has advanced to such an extent that it is now possible to discover and measure the tiniest of particles—even those that are *unseen,* such as the Higgs boson, also appropriately called the 'God particle'. We are now beginning to understand how physical properties actually become physical properties.

Irrespective of how it manifests itself, everything that exists is a vibrating bundle of energy—even if we are not aware of it with our senses. To use a simple example, we cannot hear the sound of a dog whistle. Its rate of vibration is beyond our human capacity to hear it. Yet it exists and can be measured. And dogs can certainly hear it!

Different rates of vibration produce different effects. We all know that a glass can be shattered by the sound waves of a human voice at the right vibrational level.

In the same way and for the same reason, our unseen emotions and thoughts also have their own vibrational frequency. This is how we are aware if an emotion (emotion = e-motion = energy in motion) is positive or negative, if it engenders happiness or sadness. We may not be able to see these feelings, but we certainly experience them.

We are conditioned to believe that what we read, been taught or hear from our friends and the media is the truth. We have to realize that these 'truths' are just opinions. Equally, we need to appreciate that our beliefs about what is 'definitive' are just perceptions of our senses. They are not reality or the truth when viewed in the context of a universe of vibrating quanta.

The maxim 'I'll believe it when I see it,' which we all have used at some time, should really be turned around! We should say 'I'll see it when I believe it.' This would reflect an understanding that the vast majority of what happens around us is not accessible to our human senses at all—and yet clearly exists!

When we switch on the light, we cannot *see* the connection that allows the switch to connect to the electricity source and activate the light. We do not need to know how this process works, only *believe* that it does. Experience will prove the rest. When we use our smartphone, we can call up films, music, games, buy tickets or send money. We cannot see how these miracles happen, but we believe that they do. We rapidly take them for granted, even though we have no idea how they actually work.

Every time we do anything, our body is responding to a thought that we cannot see (or access with any of our senses) yet we know that the connections exist—and work. Each of these thoughts is connected to another and another and another in a continuous process.

Similarly, the gigantic volume of energy-created activities that happen in the Universe at every second are the result of energetic 'thoughts' connected to other thoughts. We may find this a difficult concept to accept, because, in our ignorance, we assume that things we cannot 'prove' or access with our senses cannot therefore exist. We are convinced that unless something has a name and is 'scientifically verifiable', it cannot exist. We tend to rely just on our senses to instruct us on what is true and what is not true, and, thus, what we believe and don't believe. Science is still in its infancy. Every day, it is discovering new 'truths' that disprove the previous 'truths' that were fervently promulgated just before. We should always keep an open mind!

Even though we do it all the time, 'judging by appearances' has always been a rather hazardous way to make evaluations. It relies on what our five senses show us physically and on our (often erroneous) subconscious 'beliefs'. Making decisions based only on our senses or the opinions stored in our subconscious clearly limits our perspective about life and, therefore also, the outcomes we can attain.

Understanding how vibrations, frequency and energy work enables us to look at life from a different perspective. We can then take different decisions that can dramatically alter the course of our life. In the words attributed to Nikola Tesla, 'If you want to find the secrets of the universe, think in terms of energy, frequency and vibration.'

In nature, for example, plants can 'hear' energetic vibrations around them and respond to them. Researchers from Tel Aviv

University found that playing recordings of flying bees to evening primrose flowers stimulated, within three minutes, a 20% increase in the sugar concentration of these plants compared to those left in silence. 'Both the vibration and the nectar response were frequency-specific,' said Lilach Hadany, the evolutionary biologist. 'We found that the flowers vibrated mechanically in response to these sounds.'

The Japanese scientist Masaru Emoto demonstrated how human thoughts and intentions impacted water. His experiments showed how the molecular structure of water changed significantly when exposed to the different vibrational frequencies of human beings as well as music. Water appears to have a 'consciousness' that is affected by the power of human thoughts, sounds and intentions. Since human beings are made up mostly of water, the question arises as to whether we can draw health benefits from this knowledge—especially since further experiments have shown that toxins in water can be energetically neutralized.

Everything is energy in motion and vibration. Our thoughts are vibrations. Words are vibrations. Our feelings are vibrations. Our subconscious mind stores all these thoughts, memories and emotions of our past and acts as a giant library and memory bank. Everything we have ever experienced is in there somewhere. Everything in the Universe that we 'perceive' is only made so by the quality of consciousness that we hold, which is itself determined by the beliefs and expectations that we have accumulated.

Our conscious mind draws its habits, attitudes, beliefs and expectations from this pool. These attitudes become habitual. They take on a dominant vibration. This dominant vibration resonates with other similar vibrations and draws them to us and us to them.

Like attracts like.

Misery loves company!

We can also explore how we might wish to shift the vibration rate of our own thoughts, feelings and intentions in order to create different and better outcomes.

The individual consciousness that we all have, which is determined by our beliefs and attitudes to life, is constantly vibrating, through its thoughts and actions and drawing to itself the mirrored reflection of the frequency it has chosen to emit. So, if we wish to change these frequencies, we need to understand how best to do this.

We are constantly bombarded by bad news—from what we read in the papers or see on TV, but increasingly also from blogs and social media. These all press on our subconscious mind and, in the face of the apparently unending stream of unhappiness, unfairness, corruption, waste, destruction and negativity, often make us feel frustration, anger and a sense of powerlessness.

This bad news vibrates at a low frequency. It is the frequency of fear and resonates with any similarly low-frequency thoughts that it stimulates in our mind. It is then stored in our subconscious library for future reference and influences how we subsequently think.

The same is true of any criticisms or unkind thoughts that we have received from our parents, teachers, friends and peers. These remarks are negative, low-frequency messages that we have stored and have determined who we have become and how we perceive our world.

Many people view the world as an essentially difficult and unfriendly place where life is hard. They say, 'Money doesn't grow on trees,' and 'Charity begins at home.' If in our past we were surrounded by such predominantly negative people, we are likely to have assumed many of these thoughts ourselves. Our tendency will be to see more bad than good, to be suspicious rather than trusting and to act defensively rather than generously. We will assume that people are more likely to be untrustworthy than trustworthy. We have adopted the low-frequency, negative vibrations that we have received. And we are very likely to transmit these same waves out again as we go about our daily life. As we have said before:

Misery loves company!

Unless we modify these low-frequency vibrations in ourselves, from the inside, and turn them into higher-level ones, we will find that we attract more negative people and negative events into our life. These are not people who can help us—precisely because they have the same negative vibrational frequency. That's why they are drawn to us and us to them.

In some people, the negativity is so endemic that even good news is somehow always turned into bad—by innuendos, cynical comments, incredulity, and so on. We also need to be very mindful of the effect that our thoughts, actions and words have on those around us and on our Universe. Our words and actions cannot be undone. We should be very careful about every one of them. Their effects could have far-reaching consequences.

There is an old Chinese story about dropping a pebble in a pond and then trying to stop the ripples that illustrates this point.

'Drop a pebble in the pond,' the wise man told the boy, 'and watch the endless circles, as the ripples spread with joy. Then try to stop them quickly. Stop those ripples if you can and see what really happens, catching ripples with your hand.' So the boy dropped the pebble in the pond and tried to stop the ripples. 'This act is really foolish. I can't make the ripples stop! You cannot stop a ripple once you let the pebble drop.' 'Precisely,' said the wise man. 'One can't undo an action, be it good or be it bad.'

How do we learn to manage this?

The answer, as in the case of Oneness, lies inside us—in our own mind and in ourselves. It is never by seeking to work on the outside that change will happen—only on the inside. The great news is that every human being has the power within themselves to effect dramatic and lasting change. It is less a question of creating a new mindset but more of removing the blocks and conditioning that have caused the negativity in the first place.

How well do your thoughts perform on the negative vs positive dimension? How aware are you of the conditioning blocks in your life? To what extent do you take time to really consider what you are thinking and why you are thinking that way? Have you ever really become the observer of your thoughts and tracked what your subconscious is telling you and why?

When you practise and become proficient, you will find yourself smiling as you observe thoughts coming from your subconscious into your mind which, on reflection, are totally unhelpful. When you reach this stage, you are becoming *conscious*. You are awakening to the fact that you can observe your own thoughts and control them. You are not your thoughts. There is a power greater than your thinking that allows you to be the observer. That is conscious awareness.

In order to reach this level, you must first examine your own mind, feelings and thought patterns carefully and precisely.

Absolute honesty and authenticity are required. These are the questions you need to ask yourself.

Are your thoughts predominantly positive or negative? When you observe your life and your environment, do you feel that you are enthusiastic or cynical, accepting or critical? Do you see your world as a place of happiness and boundless opportunity or one that is increasingly dangerous and frightening?

Are you generous in your thoughts and deeds or are you careful about praising or giving? Do you generally live up to your promises and commitments to yourself and to others, or do you tend to take on too much, never seem to have enough time and never deliver? Do you take time to consider the feelings of others, or do you only have time for your own goals and objectives? How do you feel when you 'disappoint' and how does it feel when you 'succeed'?

Are you using your time in a valued way? Or are you wasting time on valueless activities such as surfing the web, scrolling through social media and posting selfies? Do you sometimes feel disconnected and distracted and fill the void with addictions such as gaming, eating or alcohol? Do you ever choose to spend time seeking a higher truth, praying, meditating, helping, volunteering, empathizing and sympathizing? Or do you shun these pursuits as 'unnecessary' and 'time-wasting'? Are you generally reactive to what is happening and follow the herd, or are you proactive and take steps to live your own life, irrespective of the approval of others? Can you detach yourself from the assumptions and stories that have been told about you and conditioned your thinking or are you condemned to believe that your past is who you are and cannot be changed? Are you ever truly still and silent? Are you happy in your own company, not needing other distractions? Do you ever take time to observe your thoughts before taking any action? How does that feel?

By creating space to *observe* our thoughts and feelings, we begin to understand whether we are operating at a higher or lower level of thought vibration. This is the starting point of awareness.

If we are operating on a higher level, we will be thinking clearly. We will be focused on the positive, on opportunities and solutions rather than problems. Also we will be in a relaxed state, which neuroscience has shown to be the best state for creativity. Our whole body will feel lighter. We will feel happier, more energetic, more in control, more liberated, more enthusiastic, more motivated. In spiritual terms, we will be in a state of alert consciousness—where we avoid judgment or any sense of superiority or ego boosting.

When we are operating at a higher vibrational level, we will be present in the moment. We are conscious of our internal feelings, which we acknowledge, accept and to which we surrender. There is no space for the ego to exist because the ego feeds on the negative vibrations of our time-based anxieties—frustrations and concerns about the past and worries about the fulfilment of our desires in the future. In the present moment—right now—neither past time nor future time exist. Only the present moment exists, which is the only time that we can live our life anyway. When we live in the present moment, the negative vibrations of the ego have no space in which to influence us.

At the higher vibrational level, we smile more, laugh more, are kinder and more tolerant. We achieve more, are much happier and maintain an inner calm. We're also more fun to be with! We are not so frenetic about time—so harried or hurried. We meet our commitments not because we *have* to, but because we *want* to. When we live in the moment we are One. Our soul and body are in harmony. It is a wonderful and peaceful place to be. In the words attributed to Mahatma Gandhi: 'Happiness is when what you think, what you say and what you do are in harmony.'

However, if we are operating at a lower frequency, we feel darker, heavier, unhappier and more discontented. We find it harder to concentrate, to be kind or to smile. We tend to ruminate on the past and be fearful of the future. We believe we see negative thoughts and intentions in others (a projection of our own feelings and a vicious circle that goes on repeating itself in our mind). We are more judgmental about others, gossip and spread unkind rumours. We find a lot of time to complain and seek others to complain with! Yet we 'never have enough time,' and thus fail to meet our commitments.

The result is that we are followers rather than leaders, unwilling to take responsibility for our life. Unable to set our own standards and our own truth, we instead try to live up to the expectations of others. Under such stress, we cannot live in the moment as our mind is constantly assaulted by negative thoughts and ideas. Our self-talk is compulsively negative and critical.

None of us is perfect. We will all recognize aspects of ourselves in both descriptions. That is entirely normal. However, becoming *conscious* of our thoughts enables us to recognize who we are and what our behaviour patterns are. By being aware of our thoughts, we can start to replace negative thoughts with more positive vibrations on a systematic basis. We can start to take charge of our life and set our own expectations and standards in the realization that we only become 'inferior' if that is what we allow ourselves to be.

To change your mood or mental state, change your vibration.

—*The Kybalion*

Here are some practices that can be readily adopted:

Just *thinking* about creating positive vibrations or thoughts is in itself highly beneficial and will start the process off. The more we practise thinking positive thoughts, the better and easier it becomes. Remember: we are as we think. Positive vibrations are the product of our mind and our thinking, not the other way around.

It is not external events that create positive or negative thoughts, but internal thoughts that create positive or negative events.

Whenever we *start* to feel negative, unhappy or judgmental, we first need to be aware of these feelings and acknowledge them. This is the beginning of conscious awareness. We are consciously awakening to the dictates of our ego, since all negative thoughts are ego derived. It is then for us to control our self-talk—which is nothing other than the accumulated beliefs of our ego—rather than allow our self-talk to control us. Once the existence of this negative stream of thoughts has been identified, we can then actively and consciously *stop* their flow by acknowledging them first, and then replacing them with positive visual images.

We need to anchor ourselves immediately to positive thoughts and pictures. We do this by using our imagination to conjure up a world or environment of peace and harmony, a picture that is positive and the opposite of the one that has caused us to feel despondent and negative.

There is no point in trying to refute or negate the negative thoughts because the subconscious mind cannot process a negative.

Acknowledging and accepting our thoughts as they occur reduces their power and makes them easier to replace.

We next need to close our eyes and slow down our breathing. In this calmer state, we can more easily discover why we are feeling the way we are and where these feelings are coming from. Are they concerns or anger about something in the past or fears about the future? Are they anxieties about what we may have experienced recently—when our ego may have felt attacked or belittled—or are they because we are stressed and worried about something that we are due to confront? By examining these feelings carefully and becoming an observer, we can create some detachment from them. It is only then that we can gain any understanding.

We can learn, for example, that unless these thoughts are relevant to us *right now* they are mental illusions—fanciful and negative constructs that do not exist in reality, only in our imagination, and are thus of no value to us.

> If you are pained by external things, it is not they that disturb you, but your own judgment of them. And it is in your power to wipe out that judgment now.
>
> —Marcus Aurelius, *Meditations*, Book VIII

Our thoughts are our perception only of what we are experiencing. We are making a judgment of the hurt we are feeling. They are what we *imagine* to be reality, not reality itself. They exist in *our* mind and in our mind *only* and nowhere else. They are illusions created by our mind, by our ego, in order to sustain our egoic sense of who we are. While we cannot control what happens 'externally', we *can* learn to control what happens 'internally'—that which is inside our own mind, in the present moment. The present moment is the only moment that truly exists, and it is only in the present moment that we can truly act.

Once we learn to accept either that most of our concerns are not real but illusions or that we can do nothing about them as they are outside our control and there is no point sustaining them, then they will disappear. We will be learning to let go and live in the present, in the now.

We can now change our perception and observe ourselves operating with more positive, higher-frequency images in our mind. We can visualize ourselves as a happy, positive, smiling person. By consciously changing our vibrations we will not only change our perception of the world but also the perception others have of their environment. The positive aura that we create around us will also be reflected in those around us.

As we apply this practice regularly and examine our thoughts and feelings for a few minutes every day, replacing negative feelings with positive ones and visualizing ourselves as kinder and more loving people, we will be creating a new behaviour pattern. Our subconscious mind *will* gradually and systematically adopt this as its new reality. We will have created a new belief and a new habit of replacing negative, low-frequency vibrations with positive, higher-frequency ones.

Here are several other practices that have been found useful for raising the frequency of our vibrations:

Develop our listening skills

This will enable us to create the time to think more carefully before we speak or write. If what we are about to say is at a low frequency of vibration and is negative (or potentially unkind, sarcastic or subject to a negative interpretation), then we need to rethink and rephrase. If this is likely to create hurt or anger or is in revenge for the unkindness we feel we have received, it will do no good to be negative in return. Hate was never overcome by hate.

That does not mean that we cannot or should not disagree or that we should stay silent in the face of any injustice. Of course, we can and must when we need to. However, there is a way of doing this without causing additional offence (a negative vibration) and which allows the other person to come away understanding our position but with their self-esteem and ego undamaged. This is also much more likely to achieve a beneficial result.

Meditation

This practice is highly recommended. It enables us to experience a state of calm, peace and harmony—a spiritual connection with the Universe and with Oneness—from which we can better deliver higher, happiness-inducing and positive vibrations. (The phrase 'spiritual connection with the Universe and with Oneness' should now not seem quite so weird as it might have done before reading this book.)

We need to start to accept that we are a microcosm of this beautiful world. We have to see that being one with the Universe is the foundation of peace, unity, harmony and love. Then we can also see how this relationship helps our ability to generate healthy, positive thoughts in place of negative ones.

Spend time with positive people

Find people who send out cheerful, enthusiastic, happy vibrations and who project a positive, can-do aura. They will make you feel uplifted, energized and comfortable. The vibrations of happy, enthusiastic people are the vibrations of joy.

Avoid negative images

It is wise to stay away from negative TV programmes, media or online content. Similarly, shun videogames that contain (or even reward) cruel, unkind acts of violence. All these invade our brains with their predominantly negative *images,* which we are then much more likely to adopt.

Research has shown that the consumption of negative images affects very negatively the way we feel—not only about the world but also about our fellow humans. We become angry, frightened and resentful about what we see and hear and frustrated at our helplessness. We feel diminished as human beings and experience a sense of desperation and despair. Our ego feeds on these negative images by making us fearful or superior, different or disdainful.

Learning these practices to raise our vibration levels is a liberating experience. We find ourselves being more positive and ambitious about what we can achieve, about our fellow human beings and about what we can contribute to our society, our world and the Universe.

When we experience a sense of positive energy, it draws others to us and us to other similarly minded people. We will spend more time with those we love, and we'll inevitably meet interesting people, most of whom will share the same vibrational frequency. We will find many who will be willing to help and support us—they have appeared in our life for a reason, just as we have appeared in theirs.

Above all, we will experience an immense sense of gratitude for the life we have, for our family and friends and for the beauty that surrounds us.

Thinking these thoughts alone and just saying 'thank you' will automatically raise our thought vibrations and bring us to a better, more enlightened place. We can echo the words credited to Albert Schweitzer: 'To educate yourself for the feeling of gratitude means to take nothing for granted, but to always seek out and value the kind that will stand behind the action. Nothing that is done for you is a matter of course. Everything originates in a will for the good, which is directed at you. Train yourself never to put off the word or action for the expression of gratitude.'

> There is nothing which I can esteem more highly than being and appearing grateful. For this one virtue is not only the greatest but is also the parent of all the other virtues.
>
> —Cicero, *Pro Plancio*

Years ago I had a Buddhist teacher in Thailand who would remind all his students that there was always something to be thankful for. He'd say, 'Let's rise and be thankful, for if we didn't learn a lot today, at least we may have learned a little. And if we didn't learn even a little, at least we didn't get sick. And if we did get sick, at least we didn't die. So let us all be thankful.'

—Leo Buscaglia, *Born for Love*

11
The Law of Attraction

Have you ever wondered why some people achieve results that others consider almost impossible and would not dream of attempting?

Have you noticed how success comes to some people with seemingly little effort, while others strive hard and diligently in vain?

Have you considered why some people are surrounded by wonderful friends and colleagues who have a wide range of interests, extensive knowledge of many subjects and a sense of happiness, humour and dynamism? Together, they discover and explore new opportunities and learn from each other. Meanwhile, others remain fixed in a narrow circle of friends who share the same perspectives and interests and the same rather listless existence.

Have you noticed how some people find compatible friends and partners easily? They find people in whom they have justifiable trust and confidence and with whom they find love and happiness. At the same time, others search frustratingly for long periods. They always attract the same, unsatisfactory characters with the same unfortunate outcomes.

Have you ever been aware how some people are naturally positive? They smile a lot, engage easily with anyone and are modest and humble yet attentive and alert. Such people exude kindness and authenticity and project an aura of warmth, confidence and trust. Others, however, are always cynical and critical. They complain about how unlucky they are and blame others for their misfortunes. They say, 'If only *they* would do this or that,' without ever explaining who 'they' are. Such people project an aura of uncertainty, insecurity and negativity.

If any of these observations resonate with your own experience, you have seen the Law of Attraction at work.

The Law of Attraction is directly related to the concept of *vibration.* Both concern mastering vibrational frequency in order to improve life, wellbeing and happiness for oneself and for others. However, the essential difference is that while the concept of vibration is directed at raising the level of vibrational frequency in order to project a higher level of positive intention and connect to others on a similar frequency, the Law of Attraction uses these thought vibrations specifically to attract a particular benefit.

We attract what we think. Like attracts like. If our mind can focus sufficiently powerfully on what we desire, we will attract it. What we send out into the Universe, we receive back. By focusing on positive thoughts, we can attract positive experiences into our life. Much has been written about the principle of attraction and much of it has been directed at using the law for personal, material or financial gain. This entails using visualization techniques to create detailed, vivid, emotive pictures of what you wish to gain, such as acquiring a new car, a monetary fortune or a bigger home, and then making choices and taking actions that are single-mindedly directed at that goal.

However, just like the concept of vibration, the purpose of the Law of Attraction is *not—nor was it ever*—to acquire material things. Of course, it is always possible to seek to use the law for this purpose, but that is not what it was intended for. Rather, it is a betrayal of the original idea and its true value, which is of a much higher order.

The Law of Attraction is not a tool to be used. It does not have a 'purpose' at all. The Law of Attraction simply *is*. It exists and is immutable. Indeed if it is used for personal gain or selfish intentions, the associated negative vibrations will not produce positive results. It is not possible to seek to contribute positively to the Universe while at the same time yearning for material advancement. These two objectives cannot co-exist. They are diametrically opposed.

> It is not possible to give yourself to both, to things that perish [material, transient things] and to things divine. For seeing that things that exist are both transient and divine, the man who has the will to choose is left the choice of one or the other; for it can never be both.... Now the choosing of the Better not only proves a lot wiser, seeing it makes a man to become more like God, but it also shows his piety to God. Whereas choosing the Worse destroys the man.
>
> —*Corpus Hermeticum*

A very similar thought is expressed in the New Testament:

> 'No one can serve two masters: either he will hate the one and love the other, or he will be devoted to the one and despise the other. You cannot serve God and money. Therefore I tell you, do not be anxious about your life, what

you will eat or what you will drink, nor about your body, what you will put on. Is not life more than food, and the body more than clothing?'

—Matthew 6:24

The real opportunity provided by the Law of Attraction is to enable us to connect to a higher, more spiritual force in order to attract a more enlightened understanding of the 'divine' that exists in the universe and in the self, which can then be used for the greater good.

The breeze at dawn has secrets to tell you.
Don't go back to sleep.
You must ask what you really want.
Don't go back to sleep.
People are going back and forth across the doorsill Where
the two worlds touch.
The door is round and open.
Don't go back to sleep.

—Rumi, 'The Doorsill'

By connecting to higher planes of thought we awaken to the immense possibilities that are offered by our mind, if we learn to use it properly. We have immense capabilities and power. To discover them, we have to spend time in deep thought and develop a more profound understanding of who we are, who we want to be, as well as the responsibilities we have as human beings and how to exercise them. If we want to understand and apply the Law of Attraction, we have to start by examining how we interact with the Universe and how we believe the Universe is interacting with us.

Do we believe that we have the desire, ability, creative energy and sense of responsibility to determine what happens to us? Can we *cause* things to happen and to influence their *effect*? Or do we believe that we have little influence on what really happens to us? Perhaps that we are subject to the laws of random chance, that we are the *effect* of what others *cause,* or that events are destined to just happen to us as we drift like a cork on the ocean?

If we believe that it is up to us, and us alone, to determine our future, then it follows that we need to know how to *attract* the best through our habits, beliefs and expectations. And that, in turn, means that we have to know how to establish habits that are based on goodness, kindness, compassion and love—because that is what we will gain in return.

The words of Jesus are often cited in this context:

> 'Ask and it shall be given you; seek, and ye shall find;
> knock, and it shall be opened unto you.'
>
> —Matthew 7:7–8

> 'What things soever ye desire, when ye pray, believe that ye receive them, and ye shall have them.'
>
> —Mark 11:24

These words have been used to support the contention that if we apply the Law of Attraction with determination, we can acquire great material wealth—the newest Ferrari, the beautiful home, the wonderful yacht. All we have to do, apparently, is to visualize these things with real energy and belief for them to be delivered to us.

This is a very far cry from the real meaning of Jesus' words in the Sermon on the Mount.

These words are not about achieving 'material' wealth at all—since the quest for wealth and possession is transient, inherently unstable and without real meaning—but rather they are about using reflection and prayer to find wisdom, understanding, compassion, love, respect and humility.

This is what it means when we apply the Law of Attraction in a way that is virtuous and more in keeping with its original intention. We ask for guidance in learning how to be a better person, how to show more humility and how to control ego better. We seek direction on how to be more loving, generous and compassionate.

We will attract kinder people if we treat people with kindness. We should avoid making judgments because judgments are always ego driven. They suggest we are somehow better than those we are judging. We will more easily find love and friendship if we learn to give love and friendship. Above all, if we feel comfortable with who we are and can love who we are, we will feel worthy of the love we receive.

We will attract happier, more contented, compassionate, tolerant and successful people if we learn to be more tolerant, more accepting, better listeners, kinder, gentler, more enthusiastic people ourselves.

How to create a virtuous cycle of attraction

There are a number of useful exercises that can help us to create a virtuous cycle of attraction. However, in order to do them well, our mind needs to be receptive to change. We have to fully accept that we are wholly responsible for what happens to us and for our destiny. We have to ensure that our own 'locus of control' is internal. This means we fully accept it is up to us to control how our own life will develop. Control is no longer 'external', where we think that others decide what happens to us. We have to take back our power and not give it away to anyone else. We are the masters of our fate. We have to take responsibility to *be*, before we can attempt successfully to *do*.

> We must Be before we can Do, and we can Do only to the extent which we Are, and what we Are depends upon what we think.
>
> —Charles F Haanel

Our thoughts, feelings and beliefs on this point will have a major effect on how we view the world. This, in turn, will lead us to decide to make a positive decision about what we want our life to be.

> Albert Einstein said, 'Your imagination is your preview of life's coming attraction.' And this works both positively and negatively.
>
> —Bill Glass, *Expect to Win*

What future do we want?

To create a powerful vision for our future (and our family and friends), we have to visualize it in considerable detail. What will life be like when we have achieved our vision? If we want a loving future, for example, how will it feel to be surrounded by love? What would it be to be kind and considerate, to accept others with respect and tolerance, to listen before speaking, to be humble, grateful, fun loving, understanding, pleasant to be with?

Our subconscious mind cannot tell the difference between what is 'real' and what is 'imagined'. Thus, imagining and visualizing our future vividly, as if it existed *right now*, will create an energy in us to move towards what we are seeking.

We need to be clear about who we wish to be and become as human beings ('what thing soever ye desire'), what changes we need to make to ourselves in order to achieve this and then imagine that to be our present state ('believe that ye receive them'). We have to make our future vision real *now*.

What new habits do we need to establish?

If we want to attract these positive characteristics in our life, how can we adopt them ourselves right now? Not tomorrow, or the next day; but right this minute: NOW.

Everything is within us already. All we have to do is focus with intensity and with persistence. We also have to understand the role our ego plays in establishing these new habits. Are these new habits intended to be purely self-serving, making us feel more important or in some way superior to others? Or are these new habits those that will enable us to be kinder, more compassionate and less ego-driven? If these new habits attract more successful outcomes, how is 'success' judged? Is it by the contribution we make to the Universe rather than what we selfishly take out?

Through deep reflection we will then come to understand that the realization of these new habits and new positive perspectives on the world are what 'loving ourselves' actually means. This is what is intended in the Buddhist quotation: 'You yourself, as much as anybody in the entire universe, deserve your love and affection.' It is only through accepting ourselves for who we truly are that we can become one again with the Universe. As we become more *authentic*, we can learn to love others. When we learn to love others as ourselves, we will in turn attract much more positive, happier and loving people. We often find that we help them to change as they associate with the values and goodness that we represent. They will also help us to grow and evolve.

Love is the strongest energy in the Universe. The more we give out, the more we will receive back. In order to bring more love into our life, we have to change the view we have of the world. We have to reduce our propensity to complain, blame others, judge the motives of others. Instead, we have to find more things in our life that are loving and lovable—however 'small' they might be.

As we develop more positive attitudes about the love that truly surrounds us, our energy levels and enthusiasm for life will increase. This, in turn, will bring more good vibrations into our life.

As we create more positive habits, we also have to unlearn the negative ones we have developed or been conditioned in and replace them with positive ones. We create new habitual thought patterns that become part of who we are. This becomes a new way of living.

> You cannot entertain weak, harmful, negative thoughts ten hours a day and expect to bring about beautiful, strong, harmonious conditions by ten minutes of strong, positive, creative thought.
>
> —Charles F Haanel

Make authentic, successful people your role models

Another way to change your own habits is to observe what positive, authentic, happy, 'successful', people do. How do they handle themselves in difficult situations? How do they interact with everybody? Use them as role models.

Authentic people are comfortable in themselves and are confident about who they are and what they can achieve. They have a positive belief in their abilities, while being realistic about what they don't know or are less able to do. They appreciate the Socratic paradox: 'I know that I know nothing.' This enables them to be humble enough to ask for help when they need it. (And they have the tact to ask with a smile and in a way that is sensitive and respectful.) They know they actually know very little. Thus, they are less ego-driven and more open to listening to the views of others. They are transparent, accessible and empathetic. They view knowledge and wisdom as a gift to be shared, not as a weapon to be used for personal gain.

Authentic people make many mistakes—often more than others because they attempt more and take more initiatives. What defines them, however, is that they acknowledge those mistakes and learn from them. After all, mistakes provide the best opportunities to learn. We learn more from our mistakes than we do from our successes. Life is full of challenges and always will be. That is what life is about. It is addressing these challenges with courage and resilience that enables us to grow and viewing the mistakes we make along the way as gifts of learning. If we were to spend all our life in our comfort zone, we would never evolve.

> A life spent making mistakes is not only more honourable, but more useful than a life spent doing nothing.
>
> —George Bernard Shaw

Above all, authentic people are respectful of others and polite. They do not offend in their use of language, how they dress or present themselves. They recognize, especially if they have children, the critical role they play as role models. They see children as gifts from God and the Universe, to be nurtured and loved unconditionally. This applies especially as the children go through difficult times and need the most sympathy, encouragement and protection. The authentic person's door is always open, and they invite open communication without judgment.

Authentic people are positive about the world. They realize that if anything is to change, they must be the ones to do it. No one else can do this for them. It is up to them, and them alone. It is their choice, desire and determination that will attract the right results. They do not complain or blame others. Their sense of personal responsibility and accountability is central to their approach to life. It determines and defines them. If that makes them unpopular or puts them at risk of criticism or worse, that is the price they accept for being honest about the need to challenge society to change. It is a price worth paying to create a better, more loving world and Universe.

Face your fears and challenges positively

Authentic people are courageous, without needing to be reckless. They learn how to face their fears, seeking help where necessary. No one can overcome fear for someone else. This is again entirely internal—inside each of us.

We all have limiting beliefs, which have been acquired by our conditioning and subsequent experiences. These only serve to maintain our fears, worries and concerns, and inevitably affect our ability to attract what we want. Every time we are faced with a challenge and fail to address it positively, we deepen that negative thought in our subconscious.

Every time we challenge ourselves and our fears, and overcome them, we strengthen our self-esteem and confidence. We move our subconscious from negative to positive and build our ability to attract what we need and want.

> The best way to overcome undesirable or negative thoughts and feelings is to cultivate positive ones.
>
> —William Walker Atkinson

How should we go about this? Set yourself small challenges about which we have some fear and then deliberately overcome them. It may be just speaking with a stranger. It may be gently confronting an 'unsaid' (something we know is an issue but never discuss) with a friend, colleague or partner. It may be taking the lead and speaking in front of a small group of people. It may be resolving an issue with a neighbour. Or it may be something 'simple'—yet truly frightening—such as a fear of insects and spiders.

By undertaking what is called exposure therapy (the most effective form of therapy), we can build confidence and change our 'belief' system very quickly. We only need properly and consciously to overcome our fear on a particular matter *one time* to realize that it is possible. When we succeed the fear then gradually goes away. We realize that it is purely a construct of the mind—rather than reality. The 'fear' is an idea that we acquired from our parents, friends or some other conditioning.

> The lives of all of us have been moulded largely by induction through suggestion.
>
> —William Walker Atkinson

Our expectation on such matters can change instantly each time we succeed and as we experience a new reality. This greatly enhances our confidence and, thus also, our ability to attract what we desire. Just as enthusiasm is contagious, confident people inspire confidence in others. This is expressed in the Buddhist idea: The thought manifests as the word. The word manifests as the deed. The deed develops into habit. And the habit hardens into character. So, watch the thought and its ways with care. And let it spring from love, born out of concern for all beings.

Enjoy the journey

Authentic people enjoy life. They find pleasure in many pursuits, have great curiosity and are willing to take up new challenges with energy. They do these things not because of any financial or 'external' reason, not in order to boost their ego, but because they simply love doing them. They are passionate about their purpose. The reward is in undertaking the tasks themselves. They realize that the journey is the joy. The destination is simply what happens when the journey ends, which, inevitably, becomes the start of the next one. If the steps along the journey are undertaken well, the results will take care of themselves.

The authentic person dreams big dreams. She also realizes that such dreams require action to bring to completion—if the dream is to be more than mere well-intentioned thoughts.

Authentic people look for the positive in everything—however trivial. Not surprisingly, they attract the positive back to themselves. They find beauty each day because they are looking for it. This beauty is none other than a reflection of the Universe of love and of the One of which they are a part. The outside world reflects their internal state of consciousness. This sense of the importance of love was remarkably expressed by Holocaust survivor Viktor Frankl in his famous book *Man's Search for Meaning:* 'For the first time in my life I was able to understand the meaning of the words, "The angels are lost in perpetual contemplation of an infinite glory."'

Authentic people delight in their environment and are deeply grateful for the life they are living. They recognize that even when unhappy, sad, disappointing, hurtful things happen, these are all opportunities to learn. They know the greatest learning comes from examining and taking the lessons from failure and disappointment. As the Stoic philosophers such as Epictetus said: 'It is not what happens to you, but how you react to it, that matters.'

> I said: **'Isn't it a shame that with the tremendous amount of work you have done you haven't been able to get any results?'** Edison turned on me like a flash, and with a smile replied: **'Results! Why, man, I have gotten a lot of results! I know several thousand things that won't work.'**
>
> —Walter S. Mallory recalling a conversation with Thomas Edison

Authentic people know that, in the last analysis, it really doesn't matter what happens. Our spirit is eternal, and our mortal life is transient. In the words of another Stoic, Marcus Aurelius, 'This too will pass.'

So enjoy the precious moments we have! They are all too short. Everything comes to an end sooner or later. Make the most of the wonderful gift of life. There are plenty of positive things to be thinking about and doing—not least appreciating each and every day. Take pleasure in where we are, who we are or who we are with. Discard anger and resentment and all negatively inclined ego—they are all useless sentiments—and live wonderful moments of inner peace and joy.

Relive positive events

A practical exercise, especially before going to sleep, is to think about the positive events that have happened that day and to relive them. Concentrating on such positive thoughts will crowd out any negative, ego-driven or fear- and anxiety-related chatter. This negative chatter is the source of much insomnia. The self-talk feeds on itself and overthinks issues, leading to stress-induced sleeplessness and the well-known tossing and turning.

When negative thoughts do pop into our minds at this time there is an effective technique to use:

Acknowledge the thoughts (recognize that they are there rather than fighting them directly) and then focus attention on the moment itself, on the now. This means on what is happening *right now*. For example, 'I am safe and comfortable in my bed. I am enjoying this wonderful moment, right now, of peace and tranquillity. I am floating on soft clouds. I am in my own space. I am drifting off to sleep.' Then focus only on the breath. Breathe slowly in and out. Be conscious of each breath.

By focusing on the breath, the mind has no room to introduce the worries of the day. In the now, there is no space for the ego to operate. This is crucial because it is always the ego that generates these compulsive, negative thoughts. It invades and contaminates our mind with its worries about what we have done or forgotten to do and its anxieties about what we still have to do or what might happen.

It will also be very valuable to have done a few minutes of meditation beforehand. We suggest sitting quietly and focusing on the breath and nothing else. Then slow the breath down. Again, when thoughts enter, acknowledge them (don't fight them) and then return the concentration on the breathing.

> Being aware of your breathing takes attention away from thinking and creates space. It is one way of generating consciousness.... One conscious breath is enough to make some space where before there was the uninterrupted succession of one thought after another.... Being aware of your breath forces you into the present moment—the key to all inner transformation.
>
> —Eckhart Tolle

Be thankful for what you have, you'll end up having more. If you concentrate on what you don't have, you'll never have enough.

—Oprah Winfrey

I hold gratitude within my heart for the amazing gifts of the Universe. I feel the inner calm that comes from being at peace with oneself.

—Buddhist saying

Finally, brethren, whatsoever things are true, whatsoever things are honest, whatsoever things are just, whatsoever things are pure, whatsoever things are lovely, whatsoever things are of good report, if there be any virtue, and if there be any praise, think on these things.

—Philippians 4:8

12

Action

Have you ever wondered at the level of energy and action-orientation of people who complete tasks, however challenging? Compare them with others who think and re-think, change and adjust and are never able to bring things to completion.

Have you ever been surprised how this disparity in the completion of tasks has nothing at all to do with intelligence or ability? Rather, it seems to have everything to do with passion, purpose and determination?

There is a paradox here that needs to be explained. The Law of Attraction is often portrayed to imply that simply thinking carefully about and visualizing what we want to attract will make that happen automatically. The implication here is that no *action* is necessary because the Universe will bring everything to us. Why should we bother to *do* anything?

This is not right. It would be somewhat arrogant to assume that the Universe is there simply to do our bidding. The Universe is effectively neutral towards us. It obeys its own principles of love and life. It reflects whatever positive or negative vibrations it receives. Action is required in order to move from idea to completion. We always have a choice and it is up to us to exercise that choice. We cannot just sit back and rely on divine intervention alone.

> Like beautiful flowers that have no fragrance, fine words which are not acted upon are fruitless.
>
> —The Dhammapada

The reality is that, without action, what we wish to attract will not come about. The key is in the name. The Law of Attraction contains the word 'action'. The issue is what action to take, why, how and when to take it.

> By thought, the thing you want is brought to you. By action, you receive it.
>
> —Wallace D Wattles

The Law of Attraction is not a magic tool to be used whenever we want something. It simply states that we attract what we project and what we truly seek. If we do this correctly, we send out higher-level, positive vibrations that will match those that we need and receive in return. No timeframe is defined. No task completion definition is agreed. The Universe is a receptacle for these positive vibrations that it will carry and reflect back. These reflections will bring opportunities and synchronicities (which we may mistake for serendipity). But without *action*, nothing will happen, and we will be unable to gain from the opportunities that present themselves.

In order to convert what we wish to attract from the mental world into the physical world we need to create energy to power action. We need to create a momentum that will start the process. It requires more energy to start than to continue. A body in motion will stay in motion, while a body at rest will stay at rest. We need to hoist our sails if we are to take advantage of the wind. In the words attributed to St Augustine: 'God provides the wind, but man must raise the sails.'

The first key action is to be clear in our own mind exactly what our objective is. This seems obvious, except that, without conscious attention, this step is very often ignored. Instead we just drift on, dreaming generally without purpose.

What is it precisely we want to attract? What is our vision? Have we committed it to paper? (If we haven't written it down, it is much less likely to happen.) In what way is our vision likely to create positive or negative vibrations? What does our vision entail in terms of resources, preparation and timings? In what ways are our intentions serving the greater good?

> Imagination is the first step in creation, whether in words or trifles. The mental pattern must always precede the material form.
>
> —Charles F Haanel

If what we are seeking to attract is purely selfish and self-serving (wanting *something*, or having *something*), we will be creating static objectives that have no power. If we try to use the principle of action to achieve an inflated image of ourselves, we will not succeed. Our selfish intentions will project negatively charged vibrations into the Universe and that is what we will get back. The Universe will reflect back the vibrational signals it has received.

If we try to force some sort of outcome that is selfishly beneficial to us, our thinking is likely to be based on anger, envy or fear—with our ego heavily involved. In this non-aligned state, whatever we think we are 'attracting' will be overwhelmed with negativity and simply cannot happen.

As we have said, the Law of Attraction was never intended for us to acquire material objects or ego-enhancing accolades. Nor does the way it works allow this. If what we are seeking to attract is tinged with negativity (conscious or unconscious), the Universe will know and what will come back will reflect it. We will find no pleasure in the actions we take. We may work very hard to achieve our ambitions, but our actions will be 'forced'—an unconvincing grind, a drudgery. Our energy will be dissipated and drained. We will experience stress, a function of unsatisfied ego, that will further reduce the quality of our actions. And what we do achieve in terms of material success or accolades will always leave us unsatisfied and wanting more. The ego always wants more and can never be satisfied because material things (thoughts, in this context, are also things) are by nature transient and ephemeral. They provide short-term effects, until, like a drug, the effects wear off and we need another fix.

However, we can seek to attract 'things' based on inspiration (literally 'in spirit') and enthusiasm (meaning 'God within'). We can seek the acquisition of wisdom, kindness, humility, compassion and gentleness. We can seek outcomes that contribute to our world and which are true and worthy of the Universe. Then our thoughts and feelings will be in alignment with our wishes and we will be projecting positive vibrations. These will attract the same in return and will help us. What will happen is that our positive thoughts will determine who we wish to become in a spirit of goodness. This will determine the actions we need to take. As these actions become increasingly aligned with our thoughts, and as our thoughts mirror our passion, enthusiasm and belief system, our actions will be systematically calibrated with the achievement of the outcomes we desire.

Passion and enthusiasm are high energy and have high vibrational frequencies that resonate closely with the creative power of the Universe.

Because the energy behind our actions is taken from a place of complete alignment, it is both immensely powerful and effective. The process becomes seamless and painless. The activities we then undertake no longer feel like hard work—precisely because we have passion and enthusiasm and love what we are doing. We trust the process. We are in the moment. And when we are in the moment, there is no room for ego to disrupt our thinking or doubt the outcome. Enthusiasm and ego cannot co-exist.

When we are in the present moment doing what we enjoy, it is important to recognize that it is not only the 'doing' that brings us happiness, energy and enthusiasm. It is also—and most importantly—the deep sense of Being and being alive that flows into us. In those moments, we are experiencing an intense feeling of joy. There is a divine connection to something greater than us that we can sense but find difficult to describe. This is our connection to universal intelligence, the one source. We connect to that sense of Being that is infinite and hence indescribable. This is what is animating and energizing our actions and our passion—not the other way around.

We become increasingly aware that, somehow, we are being helped along the way. We may suddenly notice that what we might previously have referred to as 'coincidences' happen with uncanny frequency and often with beneficial outcomes.

For example, we might find someone sits down beside us on a bench only to discover, as we begin a conversation, she has a significant understanding of something we are seeking to achieve and is willing to help.

There are several small but important 'actions' here. We have gone out where there are people around. That is not that unusual, but we have then started a conversation with someone who 'randomly' comes to sit next to us. We have engaged in a meaningful conversation, at the conclusion of which we have received an offer of help. We have done something that many would not bother to do at all.

> For every soul there is a guardian angel watching it.
>
> —Quran, 86:4

Similarly, we can go to new places, accept new assignments, meet new people and try new activities. All these actions will increase the likelihood of us finding what we are seeking—even though we may not know exactly what they are leading to. We will find ourselves saying 'yes' rather than 'no' to opportunities that open the door to life and to wisdom.

> Action should culminate in wisdom.
>
> —Bhagavad Gita, IV:33

If we are clear about what we want and what we want is worthy, then our energy will define our actions and will lead us in the direction we need to go. This is what is meant in the words often ascribed to Mahatma Gandhi:

> It's the action, not the fruit of the action, that's important.
> You have to do the right thing. It may not be in your power,
> may not be in your time, that there will be any fruit. But

> that doesn't mean you stop doing the right thing. You may never know what results come from your action. But if you do nothing, there will be no result.

Having decided what we want to achieve, what our vision is and having established that this vision has an enlightened objective, we must create a *burning desire* to achieve our goal. This will counteract any fears or anxieties we might have of undertaking the journey and the potentially negative gravitational pull of our comfort zone. This desire will also propel us to move to the action stage, which we need to start immediately.

> If time be of all things the most precious, wasting time must be … the greatest prodigality.
>
> —Benjamin Franklin

Three fundamental actions are now required to start the process:

- First, in order to establish what each step should be, we should start with the end in mind.
- Secondly, we should divide the overall goal into smaller, achievable steps.
- Thirdly, we should plan and prioritize carefully.

Start with the end in mind

Starting with the end in mind allows us (and indeed requires us) to be clear about the vision, which should be written down. 'Seeing' the end result, visualizing it with intensity as if it existed right now, will imprint it on our subconscious mind. It is important also to speak of our intended end state in the present tense. 'I am doing [your goal] right now. I am [my desired state] right now. This is who I am. This is what I am committed to.' Each reinforcement strengthens the subconscious mind.

The dissonance created by the impossibility of holding two opposing thoughts at the same time compels us to make a choice. Do we take the necessary actions to transmute our thoughts into physical realities? Or because our vision lacks the qualities that are needed, do we pull back? If our vision is purely egoistic, then it would be better not to start at all. The same applies if we are frightened of letting go or of failure, or if the vision is unclear and has not been properly thought through. If we don't know where we're going, any path will take us there. If we're frightened of where we're going, or lack the enthusiasm or passion, the adventure is doomed from the start and will never happen.

Conversely, if it's a vision we are truly passionate about, has been properly elaborated and sourced from goodness, then there is no question that we will proceed with ease—even though we may well not have a clear idea yet of exactly what each step will entail.

Divide the goal into achievable steps

Having started with the end in mind, we then need to work backwards and divide the project into meaningful and achievable smaller steps. Again, these will be defined in general terms, and not in infinite detail. Once we start, our creativity, which needs space, will determine the direction and detail of our work.

> The man who moves a mountain begins by carrying small stones.
>
> —Lie Zi

> The journey of a thousand miles begins with a single step.
>
> —Lao Tzu

By establishing smaller steps, the task becomes less daunting and more manageable. It is easier to see success as each milestone is achieved and enthusiasm is more easily maintained. It also has the advantage of avoiding the rigidity of having a monumental overall plan, which is bound to need to be altered.

> Take the first step in faith. You don't have to see the whole staircase. Just take the first step.
>
> —Martin Luther King Jr

Plan and prioritize

The third step is to plan and to prioritize. Planning means arranging the small steps in the right order with some clear idea of timing. Although the overall vision will have been created without a time element, now that we are addressing the specific steps, we need to be clear about what we are going to do, in what order and by when.

This will require some discipline. However, once we start and begin to reach our milestones, it will become less and less difficult.

We also need to ensure that every action is aligned to our objective and that we have the right focus. A point this story illustrates: A traveller in Ancient Greece met an old man and asked him how to get to Mount Olympus. The old man, who was none other than Socrates, replied: 'Be sure that every step takes you in that direction.'

Affording the right priority to our project is also extremely important. If we allot time to our project but then spend that time on TV, computer games or social media, the project will be delayed or may not happen at all. We live busy lives and, at the best of times, have to juggle priorities. If we do not accord our project a high enough priority or the time needed to do it properly, it will wither before it has even started. Most failed projects did not fail because they were poor projects (although, of course, this happens too) but because they were not granted the priority or the time they deserved. If we do not pay attention to the crop, it will inevitably fail.

Time needs to be allotted, maybe every day, in order to create a new habit which then becomes second nature. The effect will be cumulative. Regardless of what comes in the way and whether we feel like it or not, we need to undertake the actions we have decided.

> Motivation is what gets you started. Habit is what keeps you going.
>
> —Jim Rohn

Let's take a practical example: the writing of a book. It could even be this book.

What is the real purpose behind writing it?

Is the objective of writing this book to become a famous author? To make a lot of money? Or to be seen as an intellectual, a 'somebody' who is cleverer than their colleagues?

If any of these are the case, clearly the objective and subsequent actions will all be about ego. They will lack virtue and be unenlightened and out of alignment with the principle of Oneness, devoid of any consciousness about being one with life.

Alternatively, is the objective to share openly knowledge and wisdom that has been received? Do you believe it could help inspire, guide, inform and uplift? Will it even provoke new positive thoughts and actions and thereby enrich lives?

Our objective, therefore, is not to create an enlarged view of ourselves. We are not imagining ourselves as well-known writers or anything of the sort. Rather, this book should be a vehicle through which the wisdom and knowledge that we have been privileged to have been given flows to the benefit of others.

By considering our objective in this way, it is already enthusiastically alive within us—mentally and emotionally. It is no longer about ego or 'having' anything. It is about giving something we already have within us and we'd like to share.

While we may be the 'authors', it is very difficult to claim credit for the output. We can claim we are doing the research and writing. But at the same time, we need to have the humility to recognize that the knowledge we are transmitting is the result and a distillation of many other people's ideas, insights and advice. This is also true about all our so-called 'achievements'—if we are really honest about them. As with all achievements, they would not have happened without the help of very many others—those who have taught, supported and encouraged us and selflessly enabled us to find the time and the energy to complete the task.

We have been very fortunate to have been given and encouraged to develop gifts that enable us to *be* in alignment with universal intelligence and to *do* things for other people. For this we need to be humble and grateful.

> Gratitude opens the door to the power, the wisdom, the creativity of the universe. You open the door through gratitude.
>
> —Deepak Chopra

> Piglet noticed that even though he had a Very Small Heart, it could hold a rather large amount of Gratitude
>
> —A. A. Milne

Having created a vision and an understanding of our objective (the first fundamental action), we now need to visualize the end goal. In this case, the completion of a book about the path to inner peace through a detailed modern interpretation of the principles of life as set out in ancient texts (such as the Hermetic ones). We need to see it in our mind's eye as if it were already completed, as if it existed now.

This will stimulate and encourage us to act in order to fulfil the expectation we have of ourselves and to resolve the dissonance. And the sooner we start, the better.

Working backwards and with the end in mind, we can establish a structure for our book by thinking through how the steps fit together coherently in an iterative process. This will not be in great detail, only in outline form, but it will provide a picture of the journey during which we will encounter both the known and the unknown.

The outline will indicate the likely smaller steps, the chapters themselves, which can be further sub-divided into sections. Each chapter and section can be further refined. We identify what thoughts or activities need to be included, what quotations are appropriate, what purpose the chapter has and what message(s) need to be made clear.

We are now ready to complete the third action: to plan and prioritize our time. For this we need to work with our calendar and establish when, where and what we are going to do.

If we decide to write one page a day, we will have a sizeable book completed within a year. If we decide to devote a day a week and several hours within that day, we can achieve the same result. Whatever we decide (and it can be a combination of days and times), we have to have the discipline to do what we have set out to do—even if, on occasion, we don't feel like it.

There will be good periods and less good periods. (This is the principle of rhythm, which we will address in Chapter 14.) We must learn to rise above these in order to complete our mission. If we keep firmly in mind why we have selected this mission and we are enthusiastic and passionate about it, we will easily create a new habit that will ensure its completion. The Universe will help us.

> Discipline is the bridge between goals and accomplishment.
>
> —Jim Rohn

> To enjoy good health, to bring true happiness to one's family, to bring peace to all, one must first discipline and control one's own mind. If a man can control his mind he can find the way to Enlightenment, and all wisdom and virtue will naturally come to him.
>
> —Bukkyo Dendo Kyokai, *The Teachings of Buddha*

When you really want something, it's because that desire originated in the soul of the universe. It's your mission on earth. The soul of the universe is nourished by people's happiness. To realize one's destiny is a person's only real obligation. All things are one. And when you want something, all the universe conspires in helping you to achieve it.

—Paulo Coelho, *The Alchemist*

13

Cause and Effect

Have you ever wondered why some people never quite meet their objectives? They prefer to blame their 'bad fortune'. They say they have been deprived of some right or advantage, or simply don't have the time. Meanwhile, others are able to deliver more than was originally intended in spite of often much greater difficulties.

Have you ever thought about the real reasons why the world is in such a mess? Why do wars continue to break out? Why is pollution at an all-time high and are our oceans full of plastic? Why do the negative aspects of climate change continue to increase? Why are there such high levels of infant mortality from entirely avoidable malnutrition and are child depression and suicide rates increasing?

Have you ever considered why when facing an illness or a mundane problem we immediately address the symptoms rather than the root causes? If someone is unwell (physically or mentally), we prescribe medicines to alleviate the symptoms. The same is essentially true for an everyday problem like a malfunctioning garage door. We rarely spend the time needed to understand properly the causes of the problem. Thus, the results are destined to repeat themselves.

And this is what we do in our lives too. We repeat the same actions (material or emotional) over and over again and yet wonder why it is we get the same results. We are condemned to continue this process until we have understood the root cause of the effects we are obtaining.

Have you ever observed how some people naturally take charge, organize and lead, while others simply follow and do whatever they are asked to do? Or how some people seem to understand the 'rules of the game', while others behave (as the *Kybalion* says) like 'pawns on the checkerboard of life: They play their parts and are laid aside after the game is over'?

If any of this rings true for you, you have experienced the principle of cause and effect.

The principle of cause and effect has been called the 'principle of principles', because it encompasses and connects all the other principles in its simplicity. Ralph Waldo Emerson called it the 'law of laws' for the same reason. It has also been referred to as the principle of causality and the principle of consequences. All these names are appropriate in that they describe what the principle covers.

> Every cause has its effect; every effect has its cause; everything happens according to law; chance is but a name for law not recognized; there are many planes of causation, but nothing escapes the law.
>
> —*The Kybalion*

> 'People are always blaming circumstances for what they are. I don't believe in circumstances. The people who get on in this world are the people who get up and look for the circumstances they want, and, if they can't find them, make them.'
>
> —George Bernard Shaw,
> *Mrs Warren's Profession*

For every action there is an equal and opposite reaction.

—Newton's third law of motion

The principle of cause and effect is closely linked to the concept of action in that it represents the *cause* part. Actions cause re-actions or *effects*. Whatever we think, say or do will have an effect. The effect may be immediate, but very often, it will take time to manifest. But manifest it will—in time, in some way or form. The Law of Attraction is the link between the cause and its effect: we send out vibrations (actions) that will attract (cause) them to happen (effect).

And it is not just our actions that will cause effects. Inaction will also have effects—which is equally, if not even more important.

Our responsibilities as human beings are wholly encompassed within the principle of cause and effect as everything we think and do (or fail to do) has consequences at all levels—physical and spiritual. In the words ascribed to George Bernard Shaw: 'We are made wise not by the recollection of our past but by the responsibility for our future.'

'We reap what we sow' is a common saying. We should also add 'We cannot reap what we do not sow'—even though there might be great need of sowing!

Another expression is 'Everything happens for a reason.' In reality, we will not necessarily know what the reasons are and they are often multifaceted, complex and occur over time. But a reason or reasons there will inevitably be. There are many planes or levels of causation—spiritual, mental and physical.

Spiritual causes have instantaneous effects: we have the spiritual thought or feeling, and it exists immediately within us. Mental and physical causes have effects that happen over time and have time lags. All are encompassed within the principle of cause and effect and nothing escapes this principle.

The effects that we see are always the result of past actions. They simply are. They are the truth. They are what has occurred. They cannot be changed since we cannot change the past. We cannot control them once they have happened. They are the symptoms or effects.

Every symptom, effect and material thing that we see in the external, physical world has its origin or cause in the internal, mental world of our thoughts. Thoughts are things. Our thoughts create our 'reality'. Everything that we see around us is the result of someone's thought at some time. All the material objects that have ever been created are a result of an act of mental creativity by some human being.

The *Kybalion* states that 'the Universe is mental', and the power of the mind is infinite. Our minds are infinite in their capacity to create. Nothing is impossible, which, written differently, can read 'I'm possible!' Our thoughts create our beliefs and our beliefs drive our actions, which in turn produce our results.

If our thoughts, beliefs and actions are all aligned, we have infinite power. We can undertake actions that create the effects or results we want, as long as we have the perseverance to carry them through (and perseverance includes all those personal developments that are necessary to achieve them).

Sometimes, though, we carry contradictory beliefs. The result is that the causes we set in train through our actions also result in confused and unsatisfactory outcomes as the example below of trying to learn a language illustrates. This principle is neutral and is not there to help or hinder us. It is up to us to use it correctly. It will simply generate the effects that we have set in motion or caused. The effects are always the truth. They always reflect our true beliefs.

To understand what our beliefs really are, we need to look at the effects or results we are achieving. If the results we are achieving are not the ones we want, we need to examine our beliefs, our feelings and our thoughts carefully. We have to look again at what we are actually doing. Only actions produce effects. Why are we not getting the results we want?

To give an example, say we want to learn a new language. We believe that it is what we should be doing and have even started lessons (our belief has created an appropriate action) but we are making little progress. There could be several reasons, but it is likely we are harbouring conflicting beliefs.

We *say* we want to learn the new language, but we do not really accept the implications in terms of time and commitment. We do not understand or have interest in the grammar or even the language. And we feel uncomfortable and fearful that we will not succeed. Our subconscious mind knew all along that this would be a difficult undertaking.

One of our beliefs was that it would be nice to speak another language, so we told people and started down the road. The other (contradictory) beliefs were that we would never want to allot the time necessary and we did not have the perseverance or burning desire to change our mindset. We could not adjust our self-talk or rearrange our subconscious predisposition to accomplish the task.

If we had examined our true feelings, this would have told us immediately what our dominant belief was: that we were deeply uncomfortable with the prospect of going to classes. This sense would have been a much better indicator of our true belief than our declared verbal intention.

By examining the *result* (or effect), we come to understand that our dominant belief all along was that we really did not want to learn a new language. We discover that we had contradictory beliefs and our dominant (subconscious) belief was the root *cause* of our not progressing in our studies. We have discovered the truth by discovering the cause. This follows the Aristotelean precept that we do not know a truth without knowing a cause.

It is in our nature as human beings to put our focus, energy and attention on the symptoms, rather than on seeking to understand the underlying causes. This is simply because it is easier and requires less energy to take this (dangerous) shortcut.

Let us take an example of a cause leading to a delayed, painful effect. A dark-haired, dark brown-eyed Italian married woman, Maria, living with her dark-haired, dark brown-eyed Italian husband in southern France, had an illicit affair with a blond Norwegian man. Although it was a very short-lived affair, which both immediately regretted, the woman became pregnant. She did not tell her husband about the affair, letting him believe the baby was his. She prayed and hoped that the baby would be born with their characteristics. And the baby girl, Alessandra, was duly born with all the characteristics of the mother—not a blond hair anywhere. Maria uttered a huge (inaudible) sigh of relief. She remained silent about the baby's father.

Approximately twenty-five years later, Alessandra, now back in Italy and having married an Italian, gave birth to a little boy. He was blond with blue eyes.

Maria's brief indiscrete action had finally had its visible 'karmic' effect. Nothing escapes the principle. It simply took a little longer for the effects of Maria's actions to manifest in a physical form. They had, of course, already manifested in a mental form for Maria many years earlier, causing her pain and suffering.

Another way to look at cause and effect is to imagine a set of dominoes which have been set up around a room, weaving in and out between chairs and tables. When the first domino is pushed over, the action or cause, all the others fall over systematically and inevitably, the 'effect.' It is all very predictable. The principle of cause and effect, like Newton's law, and like every other principle is entirely predictable.

We can look at this principle from a purely physical point of view: this specific action causes this specific effect. I plant a seed in the ground, and, in time, a plant grows from the seed. The cause is the planting of the seed, the effect is the growth of a plant.

We can also look at the same activity from a more philosophical or spiritual point of view: I plant a seed because our world is a beautiful place and by doing so, I recognize my responsibility for preserving and healing it. I recognize the need to produce good food, absorb excess carbon dioxide and create a heathier environment for our children and grandchildren. By sustaining life, I am at one with life and with the Universe. The *cause* has now become my consciousness, my awareness of the fragility and precariousness of our world, the true recognition of who *I am* and my connectedness to everyone else. The *effect* is my action to plant seeds.

We have often quoted Socrates' 'an unexamined life is not worth living,' and, here again, with the principle of cause and effect, we need to examine with depth and care. We have to examine the causes that have led to the effects we see. Understanding the cause is understanding the *why*.

Japanese inventor and industrialist, Sakichi Toyoda developed a powerful problem-solving technique in the 1930s. It states that to get to the bottom of a problem you should ask (and answer) the question *why* five times.

Here is a practical example:

The machine has stopped (the 'effect').

- Why? (1) There is a jam on the conveyor belt.
- Why? (2) The conveyor belt is not calibrated with the line.
- Why? (3) The specification for the belt did not identify the measurements accurately enough.
- Why? (4) The process for ensuring specifications are correct is not rigorous enough.
- Why? (5) We have not allocated the responsibility for doing this work to anyone. No one is specifically accountable for this important task.

So the cause for the machine stoppage has now been traced back to a management issue of accountability. We could go on further and ask why? again. Each time we'd discover more about the root cause.

While this is not infallible, it is certainly a very practical way of starting to understand the complexities of causes rather than resorting to quick fixes that are unlikely to solve the issue.

This technique can also be applied to ourselves and our current state of being, to our feelings, to our sense of purpose, to our very existence. Why are we here?

Everything that exists is the result of causes that have occurred in the past. If we want to properly understand why things are the way they are right now, we have to take the time and trouble to examine the causes in detail.

Not doing this properly is tantamount to making a quick and incorrect diagnosis of a patient's illness with potentially catastrophic conclusions. The worst mistake a doctor can make is an error of diagnosis, since this will lead to the prescribing of the wrong medicine. This will not only not help cure the patient but may cause other problems and the delay could also be fatal.

Take the case of Chris. Tall, fit and strong, he was an active rugby player till the age of forty. One day, as he was on his usual five-mile run, he realized he was taking much longer to complete the course. He also felt pain at the bottom of his spine. He went to see his doctor, who made a number of tests at the conclusion of which Chris was very sadly informed that he had multiple sclerosis and would have a seriously shortened life expectancy. Three years later, he was still very much alive, but had progressively lost the feeling in his legs and had difficulty walking.

He was examined again. This time, the conclusion was that he had seriously compressed his spine playing rugby, running and through other sporting activities and this had damaged the spinal nerves. Had he been operated on at the time of the first (incorrect) diagnosis, he could have been successfully treated. It was now too late, and he would never be able to walk again. The effect of pain in his back had resulted, first time round, in an incorrect analysis of the cause. This incorrect assessment had very serious consequences.

The Greek philosophers and their successors understood this only too well and they wrote extensively on the subject.

> In all disciplines in which there is systematic knowledge of things with principles, causes or elements, it arises from a grasp of those: we think we have knowledge of a thing when we have found its primary causes and principles and followed it back to its elements.
>
> —Aristotle, *Physics* 1:1

> In all things which have a plurality of parts, and which are not a total aggregate but a whole of some sort distinct from the parts, there is some cause.
>
> —Aristotle, *Metaphysics* 8

> Happy the man who has been able to learn the causes of things.
>
> —Virgil, *Georgics* 2:490

Away from philosophy, how can we use the principle of cause and effect in our daily lives? How might we apply it to the achievement of personal objectives? Let us take the case of Julia C.

Julia C is in her late forties and is overweight. She is concerned about her appearance and this is causing her anxiety, pain and stress. She feels bad about herself and decides she needs to do something about this.

Let us examine the cause of her concern. People who are overweight tend to eat and drink more than they should, and exercise less than they should. Why is Julia C overweight? At one plane (the physical level), it is because of her consumption habit. But *why* questions need to be asked: why is she eating and drinking more than she should and why is she not exercising enough?

When questioned, she says she is very busy—with children (who are at full-time school), friends, coffee mornings, shopping—so doesn't have the time to eat proper sensible meals. She prefers to snack throughout the day.

In the evenings, exhausted from all these activities, she has no energy for exercise—even though she pays for a gym membership. She sits in front of TV with a glass or two (or three) and waits for her husband to come in.

He is very busy at work, has a long commute and is frequently late home. He is often too tired for them to have a meal or a proper conversation together at home. They discuss whatever is most urgently needed to be done, usually about the home or the children. They both collapse in bed.

Again, *why* does she eat and drink more than she should and does no exercise?

An analysis of her behaviour shows several things. She feels bad about herself because she has no real purpose to her life and is lonely. She fills her time with 'busy' activities in an attempt to cover her pain. Because she has not taken the opportunity to take charge of her life, she is letting other people (friends) and other activities (coffee mornings, shopping) take charge of her. Her husband's work schedule means she feels somewhat neglected, which, whether true or false, is her perception of reality.

All this contributes to her low self-esteem and her unhappiness. Unhappy people tend to eat and drink more. Depressed or mildly depressed people feel less motivated to exercise. The vibrations she is sending out are low and negative, attracting negative responses. The friends she is 'attracting' are most likely suffering in similar ways for similar reasons. Misery attracts misery. She is not whole and there is a deep division between her soul and her body.

With a deeper examination, we now understand a little better the real causes of Julia C being overweight. We can see how all the principles we have considered so far are directly relevant to her experience. She is sending out low-frequency *vibrations* that *attract* similar negatively charged responses. The *actions* she is taking have the *effect* of damaging her health, of which one symptom is that she is overweight.

What should Julia do now? She can do nothing about the effect—her being overweight. It is a fact and trying to address that fact will not resolve anything. But she can do something about the causes. What are her options?

She could go to the doctor and be prescribed medicine to help with her (mild) depression. This action, however, would not have the effect of removing the causes of her unhappiness or resolving any self-esteem issues. On the contrary, this would just be a palliative—a band-aid to cover the wound. Moreover, it could make the problem worse simply because the root causes have not been addressed.

She could have a conversation with her husband and tell him she feels neglected and she would like him to come home earlier. This action—effectively putting the responsibility for her pain on his shoulders—will not build her self-esteem and risks provoking an argument, making things worse. By not taking responsibility for her actions, she is adding to the problem. While his behaviour may be contributing to her unhappiness, it is in her hands to take charge of her life.

Allowing others to control how we feel means we lose our own power. She would be allowing the fear, anger and resentment of her ego to abnegate her responsibility and hand her power to someone else. While having an adult conversation at the right time with her husband will clearly be a good thing, it is not the cause of her being overweight. To think it is would be to try to change the *effect* that is being focused on, rather than addressing the real *cause*.

The cause is in her own mind and her own soul. She is the reason for her current predicament. Yes, there are other contributing factors—there always are. But the causes are all within her, and within her power to remedy.

This accords with the idea of Carl Jung that that which we do not confront in ourselves, we will meet as fate.

What should she do? If we want to achieve anything, we must focus first on the cause. The effects will take care of themselves. If we change the cause, we change the effect. For that, we have to take charge and recognize, first and foremost, that it's up to us… and no-one else. We are what we think. Our thoughts determine our future. Every aspect of our life is actively reflecting our thoughts and beliefs—not the other way around. If we consider this as an opportunity to take charge, we empower ourselves to create a new reality.

An unhealthy body is the effect of past actions. Those actions were the result of past beliefs, thoughts, words and actions that created habits. Those habits created our destiny. Our dominant habitual mental attitude, thoughts and beliefs did not serve us. We need to change them. We need to reverse the process and create new habits. The primary cause is her belief (or rather lack of belief) in herself and her low self-esteem. If an overweight body is the physical manifestation of low self-esteem, then addressing that low self-esteem should be the primary focus of attention.

However, before she can begin she needs to recognize that she has to take full responsibility and reclaim ownership of her life. No one can do that for her. She needs to appreciate that it is within her ability to make the changes she wants.

She now needs also to reframe her objectives. Initially, she wanted to reduce her weight. In fact, her real initial reason was to look more attractive—not the best reason, as it is too ego determined! Now she wants to be healthy, have more energy and feel alive. She wants to learn and contribute to society. Ultimately, she wants to *be* who she can really be, independently of anyone else, and take back her own life. She finds these objectives are much worthier than simply wanting to look good! She needs to write down all these positive reasons on paper—in the present tense. Each phrase should start with 'I am…' or 'I do….' She should read the statements to herself at least three times every day.

All thoughts are not created equal. The power of any thought is determined by how often we have it and the strength of feelings associated with it. The greater the energy behind a particular thought, the greater its ability to attract the physical outcome or effect that we want to attract. Passing, fleeting thoughts, held for a few minutes and overwhelmed by myriad other thoughts cannot succeed.

Thoughts are live, thoughts are energy. Where mind may be seen as static energy, thoughts are dynamic. Thought power is the vibrating force that is created by converting static energy into dynamic energy. Julia C needs to recognize and delight in the fact that everything is within her and that her ability to succeed is limitless and inside herself.

Next, she needs to visualize how she then *is* (in her future state) and how she feels like, having achieved her goal. This is not only in a physical sense but also emotionally. This image and the associated emotions need to be very vivid so as to permeate her subconscious mind, which, using her frequently repeated written statements, will start to create a new reality. This is the mental model: (imagination + visualization) x repetition = our new reality.

> The emotions must be called upon to give feeling to the thought so that it will take form.
>
> —Charles F Haanel

> A mental image gives you a framework upon which to work. It is like the drawing of the architect, or the map of the explorer. Think over this for a few moments until you get the idea firmly fixed in your mind.
>
> —William Walker Atkinson

Now she can start the detailed planning. Why is this so important?

The principle of cause and effect, as we have said, is neutral in the sense that it simply exists. It doesn't care whether we want to change or not, whether we have a destination in mind or not. It will deliver the effects that our actions determine.

This means that the more precise the actions and the more connected they are to the effects, the better the outcome will be. So, 'eating less' and 'exercising more' are not good enough. They are much too vague.

Instead, the actions (stated in the present tense) should read like this: 'I belong to a gym, I go on Mondays, Wednesdays and Saturday mornings. I have signed up for classes x, y and z, which provide a balance between cardiovascular exercise and strength training. I have signed up with a personal trainer for one session every week for the first 3 months. I have paid for them in advance. I have porridge for breakfast, with some fruit and nuts. I eat plenty of vegetables every day. I have regular meals. I drink a glass of wine on Saturday and Sunday only. I abstain during the week.'

How do we know these actions will work? They will work because they have worked for thousands of people before us. We have read articles, consulted specialists, talked to friends who have healthy bodies and sought help from people who know and have lived through the same experience.

By writing her actions on paper and reading them every day, the process of repetition will instil new habits, and change will happen for Julia. Some discipline will be necessary, especially at the start, but if her vision is strong enough and the desire to take charge of her life and destiny powerful enough, the process will become easier and easier. It is all in the mind. The mind is immensely powerful. We only ever use a fraction of its capacity. The universe is mental.

As Julia sees the results, her confidence builds and self-esteem increases. As her self-esteem and energy increase, so does her optimism. She begins to exude more positive vibrations, which attract more positive results. She becomes happier with herself. She is relearning to love herself even as she takes charge of her life.

What has been described here in relation to Julia C applies equally well to every aspect of our own lives and can be addressed in the same way. It is always up to *us* to decide what effects we want and what specific goals we want to achieve—whether they be our health, work, leisure, relationships or children.

We need to examine what actions are needed to produce the results and what causes achieve the desired effect. Because the principle is immutable, the results, if properly organized, are predictable and repeatable.

The example of Julia C is a relatively simple one. However, the principle applies equally to the most complex issues. The difficulty lies in studying in depth the causes that have given rise to the effects.

For example, the pollution we have created or the wider destruction of nature are the effects of past actions, but it is more difficult to understand all the causes. Similarly, we easily see the effects of all the wars that rage across the world, but the causes, being very complex, are more difficult to grasp. And when we consider the number of children who needlessly die of malnutrition every day, the causes can be hard to establish in their entirety.

Whatever the exact causes, the fact remains that most of the disasters and catastrophes are man-made—not acts of nature. They are the result of actions that, if we were to look at our collective minds as a psychiatrist would, are like those of dangerously criminal paranoid schizophrenics who would be committed to the most secure institutions that have ever existed.

And it is not just those who perpetrate these acts who are to blame but all of us. We observe what is happening from the comfort of our armchairs and allow, condone and even, unknowingly, encourage these acts through our mindless selfishness.

> If you fail to act now, history will have a record that the greatest tragedy of this period of social transition was not the strident clamour of the bad people, but the appalling silence of the good people.
>
> —Martin Luther King Jr

Whatever the specific reasons for each of these disastrous outcomes, an underlying truth exists. As Albert Einstein is quoted as saying, we cannot solve our problems with the same thinking we used when we created them. Unless we are able to evolve our thinking to a higher plane, there is no reason this trend of continual destruction will change.

With the development of technology, the catastrophes that once were produced by a group of people can now be perpetrated by just a few. The risks are thus ever greater. We live in an increasingly dangerous world. Without change, there is a certain inevitability about the result.

We absolutely must evolve the way we think! We have to understand what this higher plane of thinking is. We have to understand what Einstein was telling us.

> All evils are the effect of unconsciousness. You can alleviate the effects of unconsciousness, but you cannot eliminate them unless you eliminate their cause. True change happens within, not without.... Without a profound change in human consciousness, the world's suffering is a bottomless pit.... Empathy with someone else's pain ... needs to be balanced with a deeper realization of the eternal nature of all life and the ultimate illusion of pain. Then let your peace flow into whatever you do, and you will be working on the level of effect and cause simultaneously.
>
> —Eckhart Tolle

As we showed in Chapter 9, the concept of Oneness holds the key. Oneness recognizes that we are all part of the same universe and we are all connected and interconnected. It shows us that what one person thinks, says and does affects everyone else. This is even more in evidence today as we understand better that the actions of one country affect the well-being of others. Not recognizing this means we will continue with our selfish, ego-driven actions and their effects.

Oneness takes us to an entirely different place. This is a place of peace, where we are conscious of who we truly are, how we connect and are connected to our fellow beings. We need to awaken to a way of living that is different—free from ego or at least its control. We need a way of living where respect, compassion, liberty, tolerance and love can be allowed to exist and flourish. This is where we live in purpose—a purpose that is to be consciously aligned to the All.

To many, this may seem like a kind of impossible utopia—a beautiful idea that has no basis in reality and no chance of success. But it is not a vision of some *future*, magical, supernatural event that will come to save us all, like a 'second coming'. We can awaken *right now* to the surrendered consciousness of our connection to the One, to the Universe, to what we call God.

We have the ability right now to understand that our earth is also a heaven, if we can learn how to live differently, in the moment, in peace and in stillness. We will continue to develop this vision more fully in the following chapters.

> 'And I saw a new heaven and a new earth,' writes the biblical prophet. The foundation for a new earth is a new heaven—the awakened consciousness.... The arising of a new heaven and by implication a new earth are not future

events that are going to make us free. Nothing is *going* to make us free because only the present moment can make us free. That realization is the awakening. Awakening as a future event has no meaning because awakening is the realization of Presence.... What did Jesus tell his disciples? 'Heaven is right here in the midst of you.'

—Eckhart Tolle, *A New Earth*

And there's another country, I've heard of long ago,
Most dear to them that love her, most great to them that know;
We may not count her armies, we may not see her King;
Her fortress is a faithful heart, her pride is suffering;

And soul by soul and silently her shining bounds increase,
And her ways are ways of gentleness, and all her paths are
peace.

—Cecil Spring Rice,
'I Vow to Thee, My Country'

14

The Rhythm of Life

To everything there is a season,
and a time to every purpose under the heaven:
a time to be born, a time to die;
a time to plant, and a time to pluck up that which is planted …
a time to break down, and a time to build up;
time to weep, and a time to laugh;
a time to mourn and a time to dance; …
a time to rend and a time to sew;
a time to keep silence and a time to speak;
a time to love and a time to hate;
a time for war and a time for peace.

—Ecclesiastes 3:1–8

Have you ever noticed how life has its ups and downs, its highs and lows, its moments of happiness and its moments of sadness? How there are times when everything seems to be going well, and times when things don't seem to be working out at all?

Have you also observed how some people ride the storms of life with apparent equanimity, while others founder in despair and depression? And have you ever asked yourself the question: Why is that?

Have you seen how everything seems to have a pattern or rhythm—like a pendulum swinging from one side to another?

This applies to natural phenomena—the tide goes in and out; the sun rises and sets; the seasons come and go—as well as to 'material' things—monuments are constructed and decay; roads are built and deteriorate; cars are made and then scrapped.

It also applies at the mental level. We feel enthusiastic and discouraged. We have moments of great creativity and moments of artist's block. There are times when we feel very energized and times when we feel weary and listless. We experience sheer joy and sometimes the deepest sadness and pain.

The rhythm of life applies equally at the spiritual level. At times, we feel truly connected to the Universe and enlightened, while at other times, we allow our ego to overwhelm us with negative thoughts. We find inner peace through meditation and consciousness, only to find that peace disturbed by the incessant chattering of our mind. We feel a deep love and gratitude for the world and then we feel unhappy at the suffering and destruction that pervades it.

> Everything flows out and in; everything has its tides; all things rise and fall; the pendulum-swing manifests in everything; the measure of the swing to the right, is the measure of the swing to the left; rhythm compensates.
>
> —*The Kybalion*

The rhythm of life implies that there is a cyclic energetic pattern to everything—whether in the natural, material, mental or spiritual world. Sometimes the rhythm is rapid—immediate action leading to immediate reaction—sometimes the rhythm is played out over centuries or ages.

Everything in the Universe has its own rhythm. What goes around comes around. In the same way as everything in the Universe vibrates, everything is in constant motion that has rhythm.

Suns are created and when they reach their maximum power, they destroy themselves and become dead masses of matter, then a new solar life cycle begins.

Civilizations come and go. Economic cycles rise and fall. Governments come to power and then lose power. Products are fashionable, then unfashionable, only to become fashionable again. Living organisms are born, grow, decay and die.

Sometimes the pendulum swing is more rapid. Our moods swing from happiness ('up) to unhappiness ('down') and then to happiness again. Our feelings go from exhilaration to depression and back to exhilaration. We experience successes and then failures and then successes again. We feel inspired to creative activity and then lose the inspiration and suffer a fallow period. We suffer sickness and then recover. We feel a deep connection to universal intelligence for a while and then we lose that connection, only for us to rediscover it in due time.

There is good in everything and there is bad in everything. All mental states of human beings are subject to the principle of rhythm.

We are all subject, in our everyday life, to this rhythm. Whether we are aware of it or not, it exists. It is what the cycle of life is all about. As we saw with the principle of cause and effect, there is always a reaction to every action.

What is important to understand and be conscious of is that

this rhythm exists in our own life every day—often in different ways.

Where are you on the pendulum right now? Are you overall on an upswing or a downswing? Focusing on your working life, are you on an upswing or a downswing? What about relationships, social life, health, your enthusiasm for life or belief in the future? Even your sense of courage or fear is on a pendulum. For each of these, are you on the upswing or the downswing?

Not being conscious of this rhythm means being unaware of whether we are swimming against the tide or with it. We could be unmindful of what our body is telling us and oblivious to the risks we are taking.

For example, if we enjoy our sports and are doing well, then the likelihood is that our fitness rhythm is on the up. At some stage, however, the pendulum will move the other way. We can then go through a period where we are 'off form'. We may feel tired and suffer an injury. Our self-confidence diminishes. The pendulum is moving back.

Fighting against the rhythm means continuing to train in spite of our injury and aggravating the injury, which will simply mean that it will take longer to heal. We suffered the injury because we were tired. The effect was the injury. The cause, therefore, was overtraining leading to tiredness. To fight against the rhythm and not recognize its power is akin to trying to swim against the tide.

'Lack of form', which every sportsperson, performer and artist has experienced, is a manifestation of the pendulum swinging back (and every other 'negative' occurrence in our life is also a manifestation of this rhythm).

If we are unaware of the existence of the rhythm of life, we risk being forever subject to a dance of highs and lows over which we have no control. We will find that things go well at times and then don't go well without understanding why this might be, what we can do about it and what we can learn from it. We will be a reed blowing in the wind.

> 'What went ye out into the wilderness to see? A reed swaying in the wind?'
>
> —Matthew 11:7

As we grow in consciousness and understanding, we can also understand that we can rise above this pendulum swing rhythm and reduce, if not eliminate altogether, its negative aspects.

The pendulum will always move, but there are ways to have some control over its effects.

As we will discover when we consider the principle of correspondence, there are (at least) two general planes of existence. The principle of rhythm operates on the lower plane—the unconscious level. As long as we are unaware of its existence, and thus subject to wherever it takes us, it exists and operates in our lives, but we are unconscious of it. So we can do nothing about it.

As soon as we understand it consciously and become aware that it operates all the time, causing reactions in our mind and our body, then we can address it and its effect. We can rise above it at the higher conscious level, while it swings below us at the lower level. Then we can draw lessons from it and obviate or neutralize its effects.

Mastery and practice of the techniques for doing this enables us to overcome the effects of the downswings as well as benefit from the upswings.

The first step is to be mindful of the rhythms that exist in our life and to understand that they are a natural part of the rhythm of life. Managing the downswings does not mean resisting them. Rather, it means accepting them, letting go of any fear, understanding how they manifest themselves and acting in specific and positive ways in order to stay in the flow and work with the flow.

Those who flow as life flows know
They need no other force.

—Lao Tzu, Tao Te Ching
(rendered by Harold Witter Bynner)

We need to observe whether our pendulum is on the upswing or the downswing in any area that concerns us.

If we are on the upswing, it is important to make the most of the positive effects, while being balanced in realizing that, at some stage, the pendulum will swing back.

While we are in the positive flow, we need to be mindful of others and not allow ourselves to believe that this good trend was only the result of *our* actions. We may indeed have contributed to it by our behaviour, decisions and attitude—and it is clear that the positive vibrations we have sent out will have attracted positive outcomes—but we should not assume that we have the secret to infinite success.

Modesty and humility are essential. Gratitude for what we are experiencing is paramount. The pendulum will inevitably swing back, and we need to realize that: 'This too will pass.'

Every thought, belief, happiness, disappointment, every element of life will pass. They are all transient and ephemeral. When beautiful things happen, we should enjoy them. Understanding that everything is temporary should enhance our joy of experiencing them while we can—precisely because they are temporary.

Enjoying the upswing of the pendulum is entirely natural because that is the nature of life. The period of upswing should also be a period of learning, preparation and understanding how to address the downswing in a positive manner when it occurs. It will occur, so we have to address it, not with fear and trepidation but with conscious awareness, balance and understanding.

When our lives are in balance and we are on a pendulum upswing, we can experience positive emotions and thoughts more easily. We should seek to be conscious of these thoughts as they occur and learn to recognize them, not just intellectually, but, more importantly, emotionally.

Positive thoughts lead to positive vibrations, just as negative thoughts lead to negative vibrations. Cultivating our ability to generate positive, uplifting, universally connected thoughts is a very important habit to establish, and it is much easier to do when the pendulum is on the up and we are optimistic about ourselves. It will stand us in good stead when things turn more difficult.

We should also be mindful that generosity of time, kindness, love and patience, as well as money, is a wonderful antidote to negative emotions. When we give of ourselves to others, we experience a special kind of happiness because we are contributing positively to universal love and are sending very positive vibrations into the world. Being kind and generous to others is a definite way of limiting the negative effects of the pendulum because these positive vibrations will lift us into a higher plane and thus above the pendulum.

Similarly, undertaking activities that provide a sense of achievement while building self-esteem with modesty gives us access to the power of motivation, enthusiasm and joyfulness. These are all strong and powerful higher vibration elements with which we can master the negative cycles when they occur.

Another way to master the negative pendulum cycle is to learn that the only things we can ever truly control are our thoughts and our actions *right now*. The past has happened, and we cannot reverse it. The future lies ahead, and while we can plan and prepare for it, we can only do so in this exact present moment. Understanding what we can and, more importantly, what we *cannot* control allows us to reduce or eliminate stress, anger, worry and fear.

> Some things are within our control, and some things are not. It is only after you have faced up to this fundamental rule and learned to distinguish between what you can and can't control that inner tranquillity and outer effectiveness become possible.
>
> —Epictetus (rendered by Sharon Lebell)

We should not allow the future to create anxiety. That would be purely a construct of the mind—an illusory fear about something that may never happen—since right this second there can be no anxiety or fear. There is no future in the *now*, only the present.

Understanding the importance of the *now* and learning to let go of what we cannot control are essential aspects of the techniques to manage the negative swings when they occur. They help us to rise above the negative swings and to be more effective in our response to them.

It is when times are good that our soul will be more open to learning the skills to master our emotional and mental states. We discuss some of the ways to do this in the rest of this chapter.

Everything is energy and energy can neither be created nor destroyed. Everything vibrates at a certain rhythm. The principle of rhythm allows us to learn how to 'transmute' energy from low-energy, negative vibrations to higher-energy, more positive vibrations. This means being mindful of how the voice inside our head is talking to us. Then when negative thoughts occur, consciously substituting positive thoughts for the negative ones. However, this requires us *not* to seek to fight the negative thoughts. Our subconscious mind cannot process a negative and any attempt to do so will only strengthen the negative thoughts. We have to *acknowledge* the negative thoughts and *replace* them with positive thoughts and images.

This technique allows us to rise to the higher vibrational plane. From there, we become conscious of the rhythm of life at work and can leave the pendulum to swing below, at the lower, unconscious plane. If we remained at the lower plane, we would just be the ignorant victim of trends that we neither understand nor master.

In this way, we are able to obviate the negative side of the rhythm and remain positive by transmuting negative energy into positive energy through the strength of our will—a will to replace negative thoughts with positive ones. This practice must be honed through visualization and repetition—ideally when times are good and it is so much easier to do.

Practising this will also lead to a growing understanding of what it means to be conscious of our thoughts and feelings. We become aware of what is affecting our body and our mind and begin to understand what *presence* truly means. In time, this also leads to a better understanding of our true *purpose*, of who we really are—our real self.

Applying this technique also requires us to use and exercise our imagination. It is a divine gift.

> Your imagination is a divine gift, for with mental images you may build any condition you desire. First comes the idea, then a mental picture of that idea; these are the thought seeds that the subconscious mind uses to grow our conditions and environment.
>
> —Venice Bloodworth, *Key to Yourself*

All things exist in our individual imagination. 'Heaven' and 'hell' exist in our imagination. All that we see with our eyes may seem to be outside; but it is in fact within. It is within our own imagination, which is within our own mind.

We are what we believe. We are what we think. As I think, I am. We create the reality we live in. Our thoughts and our moods determine our future.

> The mood decides the fortunes of people, rather than the fortunes decide the mood.
>
> —Winston Churchill

To rise above the swing of the pendulum onto a higher plane of consciousness means understanding that, in the words of Jesus: 'The kingdom of God is within you,' (Luke 17:21).

When we begin to understand that what is *inside* is infinitely more important than what is *outside* (since outside is purely a reflection of inside) and that 'All things are possible to him who believes,' (Mark 9:23) then it becomes clear that it is in our power to manage the principle of rhythm. We have to have the belief in our own ability to affect our future—*whatever direction* the pendulum chooses to swing!

We can do this by using our imagination to change our present 'reality' to a new reality. We need to imagine carefully and powerfully what it will be like if what we want to change were true right now. Not tomorrow or some other time. But right now! We need to act as if it was indeed true this instant. We need to use the present moment—the now—to create our new reality. We need to reaffirm on a daily basis what we want, embrace the change positively and thus become who we want to be. In this way, our capacity for achievement is infinite.

> There is no limit to your capacity of achievement. You can
> be what you want to be, you can do what you want to do,
> by the creative power of your own thought.
>
> —Venice Bloodworth

This transmutation of negative energy into positive energy is what the Hermetic teachings refer to as the alchemy of the mind. Changing negative, low-vibration thoughts and sentiments (destructive and unhealthy for body and soul) into positive, higher vibration thoughts and feelings (constructive and good) is the equivalent of the alchemy of turning base metals into gold—only much more beneficial to the Universe and the One.

Another technique to manage the rhythm is to use the principle of polarity, which will be discussed more fully in the next chapter. In brief, the principle of polarity says that:

Everything has poles; everything has its pairs of opposites.

—*The Kybalion*

To rise above the pendulum swing, the principle of polarity can be used. For example, when we start to feel the negative pull of the pendulum, we should focus our intentions and our imagination on the *opposite pole* (which means positive thoughts) and replace the negative thoughts. By learning to focus our attention, and thus our energy, on the opposite pole from that of our negative emotion, we can raise our vibrations from lower, negative levels to higher, positive levels. Then we can rise above the negative pendulum swing that is part of the principle of rhythm. We can transmute anger to peace, hate to love, fear to calm, anxiety to stillness, resentment to acceptance, dismissal to embrace, criticism to praise. When we feel negative emotions such as anger or resentment, we need to focus our attention on the opposite pole. And since 'our thoughts determine our future,' we can change our future by changing our thoughts.

This is mental alchemy. We change, or transmute, our present reality through imagination, visualization and repetition. Our present 'reality' is only our perception of reality. It is only the truth as we see it—not as it necessarily is. By changing our perception of reality, we can change anything our mind chooses to change. That is the power of the mind.

Rhythm can be neutralized and even turned to advantage. When the pendulum appears to be moving negatively for us, we have opportunities to perform positive acts, to do good and be one with the Universe. We can rest when we are injured, learn new skills when we have a fallow period and develop new interests when we cannot exercise our main purpose. When we are forced to be sedentary, we can engage and communicate happily with our fellow human beings or be cheerful when we are sick. All of these demonstrate that we are part of the same Universe, part of the eternal light.

Rhythm can thus be seen to be a force for good. It harbours no fears for those who understand how it operates and how to rise above it.

15

The Principle of Polarity

Have you ever considered at what point darkness turns into light, heat becomes cold or East becomes West? When does night become day or black become white? Or sharp become dull?

Have you noticed how close success and failure really are? How easy it is to turn from love to hate and back again? How related war and peace are? How fear can turn into courage? Or life to death? Or heaven to hell? Or happiness to suffering?

Have you ever thought about the concept of duality? That everything has its opposite and that there are always two sides to every story?

Have you considered the idea that emotions that appear to be opposites (like love and hate) are in fact two inseparable parts of the same continuum? And that this also means you cannot have one emotion without the potential of the other?

If you have experienced any of these thoughts in your life, you have experienced the principle of polarity.

The principle of polarity says that:

> Everything is dual; everything has poles; everything has its pairs of opposites; like and unlike are the same; opposites are identical in nature, but different in degree; extremes

meet; all truths are but half-truths; all paradoxes may be reconciled.

—*The Kybalion*

We have all heard the expressions: 'There are two sides to everything,' and 'Everything is relative.' In the principle of polarity, there are indeed two sides to everything and two ends, or poles. Everything in between is relative to something else.

For example, heat and cold are not absolute but two aspects of temperature. There are many degrees of heat and cold between the poles of very hot and very cold. The degree to which we perceive that something is 'hot' or 'cold' is a judgment based on a relative appreciation. Hot and cold form a continuum. They are part of the same thing. Without heat, cold cannot exist.

Similarly, without darkness, light cannot exist. Without life, death cannot exist. Without suffering, happiness cannot exist. Without hate, love cannot exist. Without bad, good cannot exist. These apparent extremes are also often closely interlinked to each other.

Let us consider the polarity of love and hate.... Now, clinical observation shows not only that love is with unexpected regularity accompanied by hate, and not only that in human relationships hate is frequently a forerunner of love, but also that in many circumstances hate changes to love and love into hate.

—Sigmund Freud, *The Ego and the Id*

Life itself is comprised of an infinite number of elements for which poles and extremes exist. We need to know these extremes exist in our life and will always exist to some degree.

Understanding and being aware of this enables us to develop a sense of balance and relativity. Balance enables the mind to manage extremes better. Through this consciousness, when we encounter poles we can appreciate that there are many degrees of possibility between them. We don't have to remain at any extreme, as long as we know what is happening. Just being aware of this phenomenon enables us to create balance and to move positively along the continuum.

> Life is possible only when you have both good weather and bad weather, when you have both pleasure and pain, when you have both winter and summer, day and night. When you have both sadness and happiness, discomfort and comfort. Life moves between these polarities.
>
> Moving between these polarities you learn how to balance. Between these two wings you learn how to fly to the farthest star.
>
> —Osho

Let us examine the principle of polarity in its relationship to duality, love and the One.

In order to understand better how the principle of polarity functions, we need to examine 'love' and 'hate' in more depth and relate them to the principle of Oneness. This will also enable an understanding of duality, which operates at the physical and mental levels, and Oneness, which operates at the spiritual level.

The principle of polarity implies duality—there are two extremes, or poles. That the principle of polarity functions on the physical (hot v cold) and mental (suffering v happiness) levels is easy enough to comprehend.

It becomes more complicated, but very important to understand, when we consider what happens at the spiritual level. The principle of polarity does not and cannot exist in the spiritual, higher, realm because (as we have learnt from the principle of Oneness) everything there is One. By being One it cannot, by definition, be dual. It is above duality. If something is dual, it can only exist at the lower physical or mental levels.

True love is the bridge between the physical and mental levels and the spiritual level.

What does this mean? Love seems to imply duality. There is a lover on one side and something or somebody loved on the other. And this is entirely applicable at the mental and emotional level. At the spiritual level, however, where everything is One, this duality cannot exist. Then what is the meaning of love at the spiritual level. At the spiritual level, love operates in a totally different way from the way it operates dually (at the lower material and mental levels). Why is this the case and what does it mean?

At the mental and physical level, love is essentially a construct of the mind and it is transient and ephemeral in nature. It is fragile. It is an emotion (often highly charged) between two human beings, who experience a physical and emotional attachment to each other. At this stage, love is essentially about wanting and desiring, discovering and exploring, needing to become 'whole' through another. On the physical and mental level, it reflects both egos' wanting and needing. Both parties are dancing around each other and seeking to appear the way they think the other wants. On this level, they cannot be whole because they are two separate people, two halves of the whole. The search for wholeness is expressed as a very strong urge for union with the opposite energy polarity. Such a relationship, as indeed all relationships between lover and beloved, is unstable since it is based on perceptions and hopes. Unless accompanied by the spiritual dimension of love—which transcends ego and is based on Oneness—the relationship will remain fragile and difficult. The truth will emerge that lover and beloved are very different, with different needs and different egos. A relationship in which love (however romantic) *and* its opposite exist cannot be true love. Love has no opposite. Where there is also recrimination, anger, emotional violence or disappointment that is not true love.

> Love possesses not, nor will it be possessed;
> For love is sufficient unto love.
>
> —Khalil Gibran

Such a relationship can only really be a form of addictive clinging to an image of the ideal partner and a search for ego satisfaction and wholeness.

This may all be manageable if both partners have high levels of tolerance, acceptance and understanding, as well as emotional intelligence (EQ). The reason so many relationships break down, however, is because without a more spiritual element the different egos of the partners surface very quickly. With both egos' differing levels of conditioning, needs and expectations, the relationship can become overwhelming and intolerable. What appeared to be idyllic in the early glow of the dance turns out to be very different as the light of truth emerges.

There comes a time when a partner behaves in ways that fails to meet the other's needs and then the initial euphoria and excitement of the relationship turns to confusion, unhappiness, pain and a feeling of being unfulfilled. Salvation was sought in a mind construct about how the partner should or should not behave towards us. This is ego territory—co-dependency, judgment, clinging, mind identification—where we seek the answer to our problems through the fantasy of the ideal partner, one created by our egoic mind. This is not real. And it is not love.

At the spiritual level, however, where all is one, Love is sacred and divine. It is not about two people (duality), but about a fusion of the two into One, into eternal truth and infinite beauty. At the romantic level, partners can have a brief glimpse of this bliss when they unite sexually as one. It is the deepest and most satisfying experience that can be achieved at the physical level. It is an act of complete surrender and acceptance of the other. This is a tantalizing glimpse of wholeness and of spiritual heaven. But it is short-lived because the end of duality cannot be found at this physical level. Only in the much deeper, spiritual dimension of ego-free presence can true love be discovered.

For this dimension to be accessed, both partners must understand, respect and love each other without judgment, disharmony or ego. They must accept all differences totally and be on the same spiritual journey together. This is about acceptance by both partners of the other's *being* in its widest sense. It is about listening and expressing how one feels openly without accusing, defending or attacking. It is not about trying to satisfy ego needs but about reflecting a sense of love that is deep within. This love is *beyond* ego and beyond mind games or mind identification. It is a fusion of the essence of two beings at the deepest level. It has a sacred depth that is part of who we truly are. We are part of the one state of being, which is love itself.

To access the spiritual requires both partners to understand and have found the depth of their being. They need to feel deeply the existence of the eternal light within themselves.

In this way, love can be seen to create the bridge between the physical and mental state and the spiritual state.

> God is the One life in and beyond countless forms of life.
> *Love implies duality: lover and beloved, subject and object.*
> *So love is the recognition of Oneness in the world of duality.*
> This is the birth of God into the world of form. Love makes the world less worldly, less dense, more transparent to the divine dimension, the light of consciousness itself.
>
> —Eckhart Tolle

> Love is a state of Being. Your love is not outside; it is deep within you. You can never lose it, and it cannot leave you. It is not dependent on some other body, some external form.
>
> —Eckhart Tolle

At the spiritual level where everything is One, God (or whatever name one wishes to give the eternal, universal light or the conscious Being) is above all dualities. Since we are a microcosm of that all-powerful universal light, it means that we, too, can also rise above the principle of polarity. By focusing our thoughts, actions, attention and energy on what is good and positive, and on the spiritual dimension of love, we can master the principle of polarity and use it to our advantage.

In order to master fully the principle of polarity in all its complexity, first we need to learn to examine carefully and with proper awareness our thoughts and the emotions that emanate from those thoughts. *Understanding and becoming* conscious *of our emotions and the thoughts that give rise to them is the key not only to controlling them better but also to master the principle.*

Once we have learnt to control our thoughts and emotions, we can then apply the principle of polarity to any situation we may encounter. We can shift those thoughts from a more negative position on the continuum to a more positive one. We are then in a much better position to learn the lessons that the principle provides. We can make a friend of it—rather than resisting it.

The principle of polarity is an excellent teacher. We need the principle of polarity to show us what, for example, failure is. Only then can we properly appreciate its opposite: success. At the same time, we need to recognize that failures are only 'negative' if that is how we perceive them to be. Failure is often the best way to learn and grow. Without failure, we risk making a bigger mistake later on!

We must face our own mortality (either directly or through the death of a close relative) to truly appreciate life itself and to see how transient and unpredictable it is. We need to experience suffering in order to appreciate happiness. We need to experience stress in order to appreciate the healing power of stillness and inner peace. We need to learn that 'losing' is valuable for motivating us to do better. Through it we develop humility and acknowledge and applaud the skill of others. Meanwhile, winning should lead to magnanimity and respect for the losers. The law of polarity also teaches that negativity of any sort is ultimately self-destructive. Negativity creates heavy, low-level vibrations that will come back to us in like manner. It perpetuates suffering for us and for others.

Who really wants to be like the negative person we encounter? There will, of course, be a reason for their negativity. We should always appreciate that they will have their own story and feel deep compassion towards them. But their negativity— whatever the underlying circumstance—is a product of their mind. It is *their* perception of events. It is entirely self-induced. If they do not know or understand the principle of polarity, they will not know either how to manage negative events when they occur or their own negativity. If they then start to assume that negativity is their normal state, before long they will be so associated with it that it will *become* the person they think they are. At this point, they will have lost much of their power to change. They will not be able to recognize the upswing of the pendulum when it occurs. They will remain at the wrong end of the pole.

When, therefore, we feel negative (for whatever reason) we need to learn to focus our energy forcibly on the *opposite* polarity. We need to focus deeply on positive thoughts, leading to positive emotions and actions.

> To destroy an undesirable rate of mental vibration, put into operation the Principle of Polarity and concentrate upon the opposite pole to that which you desire to suppress. Kill out the undesirable by changing its polarity'.
>
> —*The Kybalion*

Like the other principles, the principle of polarity is neither positively or negatively disposed towards us. It does not exist to help or hinder us. It simply *is*. It is up to us to understand how it operates and learn to manage and draw benefit from it.

When we focus our attention on the opposite polarity to the negative one that we are currently experiencing, we create tension. And this generates energy behind our thoughts, emotions and actions. That energy enables us to act and make change happen. It is the catalyst for action.

> But there is no energy unless there is a tension of opposites; hence it is necessary to discover the opposite to the attitude of the conscious mind.
>
> —Carl Jung

How else can we rise above the principle of polarity and apply the learnings to our life?

An important aspect to recognize is that the principle is not about absolutes, but about relativity. There is no such thing as absolute 'courage' or absolute 'fear', the way there is no absolute heat or absolute cold. They are all part of a continuum and we can navigate anywhere along that continuum.

Negative thoughts can become relatively less negative and gradually more positive until they become very enthusiastic and joyful. We do not need to go from one extreme to the other. By raising the vibration of any thought or any emotion, we can step up to a higher more positive level. Just moving a little in the right direction will be beneficial and will give hope that much more can be achieved.

> Take the case of the fearful man. By raising his mental vibrations along the line of Fear-Courage, he can be filled with the highest degree of Courage and Fearlessness.
>
> —*The Kybalion*

Thoughts and their accompanying emotions are part of our psychological condition. We will always have to confront negative events and negative emotions, just as we will also enjoy positive events and positive emotions. Our life will always have its challenges. That is what life is all about. The issue is how we learn to deal with these challenges.

Applying the principle of polarity is not a recipe for finding eternal happiness or eliminating all suffering and hardships. Nor should it be. If we were to eliminate sadness, we would also have to eliminate happiness—since both are on the same continuum. There will be times when we will be sad and times when we will be happy. Applying the principle is an opportunity to understand better who we are and to grow. It is a way to become a better human being as we learn to transmute a negative thought or emotion into a more positive one. Positive or negative, each experience is always an opportunity to understand, learn and grow. We need to learn to change our *perception* of the events that come into our life and view them as opportunities to learn rather than occurrences to be fearful of or stressed about. Then we are on the way to learning how to apply the principle of polarity.

> Words don't teach. It's life experience that teaches.
>
> —Abraham Hicks

At no time should we allow ourselves to become swamped in negativity. There is a tendency in human beings, stimulated by the ego, to wallow in negativity. People can even perversely 'enjoy' being negative, complaining, moaning and gossiping. It can become our way of gaining attention, of provoking responses and stimulating negative thoughts about others. We can become a disapproving *somebody*, who seeks to appear 'superior' by being in the know.

There is a great temptation to stay in negativity when we believe the world is conspiring against us and that we always seem to suffer 'bad luck' while others seem to enjoy success. But if we stay too long in negativity, it becomes increasingly difficult to come back to positivity. What starts off as an occasional event becomes a habit. It then becomes *who we think we are*. We become that person.

For example, people with an illness or chronic aches and pains often allow themselves to be associated with their illnesses. They become the 'poor me' and end up being unable to think or talk about anything else. Their subconscious or unconscious mind assumes that this is how they wish to be and keeps them there. It may also be the way in which they receive the attention their ego craves and gives them an apparent status in life that they have hitherto not enjoyed.

Choosing such a negative image is choosing the extreme negative pole. And staying there simply results in continuous suffering. What we need is to use the poles wisely by applying balance and common sense to our decisions.

> Don't avoid extremes, and don't choose any one extreme. Remain available to both the polarities—that is the art, the secret of balancing.
>
> —Osho

We need to understand that our thoughts and emotions come from our unconscious mind and our ego.

Ultimately, the key to learning how to rise above the principle of polarity is to understand how our thoughts and emotions come about. Our emotions are the product of our thoughts. A thought enters our head and it triggers an emotion, which we feel in our body. Our emotions and thoughts are the product of our unconscious mind. Our unconscious mind is a product of our ego.

Our ego has developed over the course of our life. It controls what and how we think by continuously feeding our mind. It does this relentlessly. It is often referred to as our 'self-talk'. It is that little voice that is constantly chatting to us and spends so much time swamping us in an endless stream of thoughts. Our thinking is compulsive and incessant. We often find it very difficult to stop its flow and it overwhelms us. That is why we stay awake at night. That is why we feel stressed. That is why we worry about what we didn't do yesterday and fret about what might happen tomorrow.

Like the subconscious mind, our ego reflects all our past experiences and conditioning. It seeks to protect and defend itself and keep us 'whole'. It does this in accordance with the image it has of us—an image we have *assumed* over time. That self-image is a construct of the ego and is based on fiction not fact, on illusion and hope not on reality. We, or rather our ego, creates a picture of ourselves. This image has been formed over many years and we associate with who we are. It becomes our identity.

We define ourselves based on this image and this is the identity that is embedded in our ego. This image of ourselves that we hold in our unconscious is just that: an image, an idea, a fantasy. It is pure illusion and delusion. Yet we like to believe the stories our ego narrates, and we then *associate* ourselves with this completely artificially created picture. We believe our own advertising. This is of course *not* who we are—only a fanciful perception of who we might perhaps like to be or be seen to be. The greatest mistake we make is to believe this fictional story. When we believe this image and associate ourselves with it, we are in for a rude awakening when the truth emerges. We are bound to fail. The way anything is bound to fail if it is based on a falsehood.

And yet our ego will seek to defend itself furiously against any attack or slight that might aggress this image. It will seek to perpetuate the myth at all costs—even if this means lying, arguing, abandoning friends, ignoring family or even physically fighting. It does this because it believes that if it does not preserve its image, it will perish. If we lose the battle, we lose our image. If we are so associated with the image that we *believe the image is who we are*, then losing our image is losing who we are. It means losing our identity, which is a kind of death.

The ego feeds on conflict. It uses negative thoughts about what has happened in the past and might happen in the future to create anxiety, fear and anger. Stress and suffering follow. When something happens, our mind makes a judgment of that event based on our perception, which is the product of all our past thinking and conditioning. Our perception is just that. It is a perception, a judgment that is often, indeed mostly, erroneous. It is not the truth, only the truth as we *perceive* it to be.

When we think that we are right and associate ourselves—as the ego will have us do—with that perception, we defend ourselves against any contrary opinion. It does not matter how wrong our thought is or what the situation is. Sometimes we will defend ourselves whatever the cost. Our mind has triggered an emotional reaction and our emotions take over. We become frustrated, resentful and angry leading to inevitable pain and suffering.

Our angry mind may then go further and start to create thoughts of revenge, of how to regain the upper hand and to re-establish our self-image. It will work out how to be right and make the other person wrong—a fundamental characteristic of ego. This is how fights begin. This is how wars happen. I am right, and you are wrong. My religion is the only true one and yours is wrong. My political belief is right and yours is wrong. My country is in the right and you are in the wrong. I am separate from you and I feel threatened. Maybe if I eliminate the threat, all will be well. In this way, the collective ego can be more damaging than the individual—and even less controllable.

Once we identify with negative thoughts, we don't want to let them go. We will even sabotage positive opportunities for mediation in order to defend and protect our assumed position. We feel we cannot be seen to have been defeated, even if this means total obliteration.

If we want to use the principle of polarity to transmute negative thought into positive ones—to move from one end of the pole to the other—we need to understand thoroughly the significant role our ego is playing. And how to control the thoughts that our ego is projecting into our mind.

Unless we control our ego, it will control us and we will be powerless to manage our own thoughts. We will be unconscious of why we are behaving the way we are and hence unable to change. We will not even know that this is happening at all. Becoming aware of ego is the beginning of conscious awakening.

In order to become consciously aware of our ego and our thoughts, we first need to *create space and stillness between ourselves and our thoughts*. This will allow us to be able to break the incessant flow of thoughts flooding our brain. We need to allow some time for objectivity to occur—to be able to think straight!

Only by creating some distance can we start to become better aware of our thoughts and emotions as they happen. Only then can we control them *before* they develop into ill-advised actions. This requires practice in order to create competence. But it can be done and is the ultimate key to success.

It is a lot easier to practise this when things are going well and very difficult when they are not. So we should first practise the techniques when times are easier. If we want to have any chance of mastering the principle of polarity, we have to learn to become conscious of our thoughts (especially our negative thoughts) and establish a more rational perspective. We need to understand the irrationality of negativity.

Our ego believes that it can manipulatively obtain what it wants through negativity and conflict, for example, by persuading somebody else to change through fear and intimidation. But in reality, negativity promotes the exact opposite. Coercion and subjugation go against natural law and perpetuate conflict. They foment resentment and anger and a continuous vicious cycle.

Negativity never works, even if it appears to achieve a short-term result. The negative vibrations emitted will come back to us in some way—either immediately by provoking a similar response in the person or later by other means.

Negativity and negative thoughts are also undesirable because they stop positive thoughts and outcomes from happening.

The only beneficiary of the resultant suffering is the ego, which is strengthened by conflict.

We need to learn to disassociate from our thoughts.

We become disassociated from our thoughts and emotions by becoming aware of them and then we can distance ourselves from them.

A very useful technique to start to observe our thoughts and emotions is simply to take several deep breaths while concentrating on the breath and nothing else. The objective is to stop the constant flow of thoughts and clear the mind. Simply observing a tree or any object *without judgment*, helps to still the mind. We can just stare at it for a short time, without giving it a label. If we do this correctly, we become thought free. By clearing our mind and creating space, we can start to examine our thoughts and emotions when they occur. We become their observer.

For example, say we feel we have been wronged or ignored, we will *feel* this as an emotion in our body. We need to note this change and become aware that it is happening. Our temperature may rise. We may feel uncomfortable in the pit of our stomach. Our palms may become a little sweaty. There are several physical reactions that we will experience—all of them related to the stress caused by our perception of the event. Our body is reacting to the negative emotion that has been created by our mind, which, in turn, has been triggered by our ego.

Being observant and becoming conscious of this automatically reduces its impact and gives us an opportunity to exercise some control over the thought itself. We can then acknowledge it and *transmute* the negative thought into a more positive one. We are now moving along the continuum towards the more positive pole.

This requires practice. On a regular basis, even when we are simply out for a walk or having a meal, we need to consciously stop our train of thoughts and become the *observer* of our thoughts. We need to be conscious of the thoughts that are coming into our mind and recognize that this is happening. We may then even smile at our thoughts as they occur as we start to recognize our patterns of behaviour. They have, after all, been with us for a very long time.

Since we *can* observe our thoughts objectively as they happen, it becomes clear that we are *not* our thoughts. We are the 'awareness' having these thoughts, but who is now separate from them.

We only *become* our thoughts when we automatically, unconsciously associate ourselves with them. Of course, for most of us this is most of the time. When we are unconscious of our thoughts and are led by them as they happen our ego is controlling us—rather than the other way around.

By becoming an observer of what is going on inside our mind and examining carefully how we feel (our emotions) and what we are thinking (our thoughts) and where they are coming from (negative=ego, positive=egoless) we start to establish a control mechanism to *override* the negative tendency of the ego and replace it with positive thoughts.

As soon as we become conscious of the negative thoughts and see them for what they are, they lose their potency and venom. When we become aware of them, we can transform them. Whatever may have triggered them in the first place is no longer threatening. If there is no threat, there is no conflict and hence no need for resistance. The ego cannot exist with non-resistance and the absence of conflict. It cannot exist with awareness of its manipulations.

Awareness implies being present, being conscious, being fully mindful of what is happening. This allows negative thoughts to be transmuted into positive ones. This is the Hermetic *alchemy of the mind*. This is how to use the principle of polarity. By creating space to observe, understand and identify the thought and emotion and where they are coming from, we have created space to neutralise them by replacing them with positive ones.

Here's an example: Imagine you are driving on the motorway at 70 mph in the fast lane. There are cars in the middle and slower lanes and you are travelling faster than they are. In your rear-view mirror, you see a white van travelling very fast towards you. There are cars on the inside of you, so you cannot move over. The van driver comes up very close to the back of your car ('tailgating') and, after a few seconds, flashes his headlights at you.

What is going on here and how to respond? The van driver's ego is telling the van driver: 'You're in a hurry,' (whether he is or not is immaterial); 'You're an excellent driver,' (ditto); 'Some idiot is hogging the fast lane,' (saying the van driver is therefore better than you are—a classic ego position); 'They should pull over to let me through,' (the van driver is more important and more savvy than you—more ego food); 'Show him the error of his ways by flashing your headlights. Frighten him by driving up close so he gets out of *my* way.'

The van driver's ego has taken over and the van driver has associated himself entirely with the ego's narrative. Body temperature has risen, muscles are tense and his mind is in stress with a tinge of anger. There is no detachment from the mind or the emotions, which are running high. Under such circumstances, the brain's capacity to operate properly and make rational decisions is seriously impaired. Rationality has disappeared. Any notion of danger or safety has been overwhelmed by the negative, aggressive thoughts dominating the emotions, which have been created by the mind in response to the ego. The van driver believes himself to be in the right and although this is a complete illusion, it is one with potentially lethal consequences. The risk of an accident is very high.

When something like this happens, and our ego feels aggressed in this way, it will automatically seek to defend itself. It realizes rapidly that another ego is trying to belittle it, to intimidate it, to win the battle and destroy it.

The 'natural', unconscious reaction of your ego in the driving situation would be to say to you: 'Don't tolerate any of this;' 'No one has the right to intimidate you;' 'You were driving at the speed limit;' 'You are a good driver;' You can't move over;' 'You're in the right and the dangerous idiot behind is in the wrong!'

As the temperature rises, there's a rush of blood to the head and rationality disappears—only this time it's yours! And your ego takes over. This is how road rage starts, which is entirely the result of egos running out of control and overwhelming the mind. There's nothing egos like more than a good fight. Conflict and fighting are the energy of the ego.

If you are not extremely careful, your next actions may be disastrous. You may decide to slow down, to put your hazard lights on, to make offensive signs, or even worse, to put the brakes on. The risk of a fatal accident has grown exponentially and could also involve other nearby cars and their families and children. But neither driver is in a mental state to appreciate any of this. All their egos want is to win—at any cost!

And all for what? In order to defend an illusion of an idea created by the ego, based on the image we have assumed about who we are and our own self-importance! Lives are put at risk for nothing.

It is all a falsehood and ultimately valueless. You neither know the van driver nor do you care. He doesn't know you either! What is the point? There is none. It is pure insanity.

How should you respond correctly then?

Very simple: avoid reacting instantly and move over as rapidly as possible.

We can learn to ignore provocations by letting them go *right through us*—as if we were transparent—and without them affecting us. We do this in part by being aware of the futility of what is happening. We also learn to control our thoughts and emotions by being aware of them and the physical effects they are having on our body. By providing no resistance, our ego has nowhere to go. It cannot provoke us to a reaction (which it would love to do) if we are not resisting the attack. Non-resistance means non-association and creates a space for rational thought.

In this example, you need to fill your mind with the positive notion that the van driver is in a hurry and means no harm. Know it is his ego that is driving and not the person himself. He is not who he would normally be. You should imagine him as a kind person—he may be a father with a family of his own. He has no enmity towards you personally, since he doesn't even know who you are. If all goes well, which it will because you are taking the actions to make it so, it will all be forgotten anyway in a few minutes. And the risk of a serious accident will have been averted.

Is it difficult to imagine doing this? Is it really that hard to practise this technique? Begin with small incidents first and then move on to larger ones. Know that it will work and will save you from unnecessary anger and stress, which are bad for the body.

This technique of examining and being conscious of our thoughts when small irritations occur and then turning those negative thoughts and emotions into positive ones always works to our benefit and the benefit of others. It just needs a little practice. And it applies to major traumatic, life-threatening events just as much as it does to little irritations.

> I became disgusted with the state of affairs which compelled me, daily and hourly, to think of only such trivial things. I forced my thoughts to turn to another subject. Suddenly I saw myself standing on the platform of a well-lit, warm and pleasant lecture room.... I was giving a lecture on the psychology of the concentration camp.... By this method I succeeded somehow in rising above the situation, above the suffering of the moment, and I observed them as if they were already in the past.
>
> —Viktor Frankl, *Man's Search for Meaning*

This is the principle of polarity in action.

Another exercise is to see whether we can avoid 'judging' for a period of time. That is to say, whether we can observe within ourselves to what extent the thoughts that we are generating are free of any judgment. Try this for half an hour and see what happens. Count the number of times your thoughts contain judgments.

A further exercise is to do the same thing but look out for 'negative' thoughts, which include criticism, complaints or cynicism. Try this for half an hour and see what happens.

There was an exercise of this nature done during a business

workshop. The test was to see for how long the group could work before the first 'put-down' (a comment tinged with negativity, directly or indirectly implicating someone else) took place. It was also agreed for every put-down the perpetrator would put a dollar on a tray in the middle of the table.

It took less than a minute before the first dollar appeared! And the exercise had to be stopped after twenty minutes because the participants had run out of ready funds!

The purpose of these exercises is to enable us to become observers and to understand what it feels like to be detached from our thoughts. By doing this, we create space between our thoughts and subsequent emotive reactions. We can only do this by focusing on the present moment—on what is happening in our mind right now—which is not something we are accustomed to doing in our busy life.

Another way to create this stress-free, healthy space of peace is through meditation. Meditation does not have to take long or be complicated. This is not an intellectual exercise. It is an emotional one—one of feeling.

Sit comfortably in a quiet place on a chair. Close your eyes. Focus on your breathing.

As thoughts start to pop up, acknowledge them without any resistance and go back to focusing on your breathing. Your mind will gradually empty itself of thoughts. Move your focus to your hands. Feel the energy of your hands. They will start to tingle. Enjoy the sensation. Gradually move your focus to your feet. And then slowly to the rest of your body. You will start to feel your body's energy and enjoy the feeling. If you reach this stage, you have done well.

> Controlling the breath, and thus calming the nerves, is a prerequisite to controlling the mind and the body.
>
> —Swami Rama

Initially, this may be far enough, but you can go deeper. As you deepen the feeling, you will become increasingly aware of your body's essential energy. Keep going deeper. In time, you will no longer be aware of what is outside—all your feelings will be inside. You have reached a depth where you can experience your *presence.* It is who you are. It is indescribable and defies words. It is a place of peace, gratitude and love. It is where you and the One fuse. It is beauty.

By creating space to observe our thoughts, we also learn how to transmute negatives into positives. We learn to make a friend of the principle of polarity and apply its lessons beneficially. The poles may appear to be apart, but they are not only very close but totally interlinked—as are all the principles. The idea that extreme poles are different when in fact they are the same is a paradox. But it is easily resolved once we understand its true nature. Khalil Gibran explains this in *The Prophet* with deep insight:

> When you are joyous, look deep into your heart and you shall find it is only that which has given you sorrow that is giving you joy.
> When you are sorrowful, look again in your heart, and you shall see that in truth, you are weeping for that which has been your delight.
> Some of you say, 'Joy is greater than sorrow,' and others say, 'Nay sorrow is the greater.'

But I say unto you, they are inseparable.
Together they come, and when one sits with you at your board, remember that the other is asleep upon your bed.

One of the greatest meditations that should be mastered is to see the Light within emanating from every part of the body. When this can be accomplished successfully, and the mind can hold this thought for an extended period of time, consciousness will expand. Light is the great purifier of the universe.

16

The Principle of Correspondence

Have you ever considered that the state of our external world, the world we live in, is a direct reflection and a result of our individual and collective inner thoughts?

Have you reflected on how it is that the quality and development of everything that touches and affects us are all a direct result of our own thoughts, habits, beliefs and actions? This includes the people we know, our friends, relationships and children, as well as our ambitions, careers and even our state of health.

Do you recognize that there is no such thing as a chance event, a random occasion or act of 'fate'? Do you see that everything that appears to be a coincidence is in fact the result of an action or a thought that we have taken? That we have created this specific event?

The principle of correspondence states that:

> Just as a knowledge of the Principles of Geometry enables man to measure distant suns and their movements…so a knowledge of the Principle of Correspondence enables man to reason intelligently from the Known to the Unknown. Studying the monad, he understands the archangel.
>
> —*The Kybalion*

The principle of correspondence is, in many respects, the principle that holds all the other principles together. It allows us to better understand the workings of all the principles on different levels—the physical, the mental and the spiritual.

It provides us with insights on the entire process and unlocks the mystery of the 'known' and the 'unknown'. What does this mean?

As its name implies, the principle of correspondence makes clear that everything—seen or unseen—is related to everything else. Everything *corresponds* to everything else and on every level. Everything is also in perfect harmony and in balance. What happens on one level—physical, mental or spiritual—will have an effect on every level. In the words of Hermetic philosophy that we have already quoted: 'As above, so below: as below, so above.' Or in Christianity, '...on earth as it is in Heaven.' Nothing exists in isolation. We are part of the world and the world is part of us. Other people are a part of us and we are part of them. The world around us can be imagined as being holographic: each cell within us is a microcosm of the whole, just as the whole is a macrocosm of each cell. At the subatomic level, everything including ourselves, are just tiny pieces of energy, interrelated and correlated.

This means that we cannot operate as separate beings, however much we try. All that creates is conflict, pain, stress and suffering—since separateness cannot work. It is contrary to the principle. It is a condition and conditioned part of our human ego that we seek to make ourselves 'special', meaning different and, therefore, superior.

This attempt at separateness and superiority does not serve us nor does it serve the Universe. It is an essentially negative thought that will inevitably find its reflection everywhere else and will come back to us in like measure. The Universe, the One, is constantly in harmony and in balance—that is the principle of Oneness. Any imbalance that we create will provoke an equal and opposite reaction in the Universe and so to ourselves.

Everything we believe, say and do affects everything else immediately—whether we like it or not. The Universe reflects what we believe: 'As within, so without.'

Our outer world is always a reflection of our inner perceptions and not the other way around. The world we inhabit is entirely the product of our thoughts, imaginings, prejudices, beliefs and expectations. It is the result of the actions that emanate from our thoughts (either individually or collectively) and we have to take responsibility for them and their effect.

When we are born, we are born *pure*, in the image of God. While inherited genetic features will clearly predispose us to certain physical and mental characteristics, we have no innate habits, attitudes, beliefs and expectations. We have no perceptions of the world around us. In our innocence, we are the children of God and 'of such is the kingdom of Heaven'.

As we grow up and develop, so does our mind. We learn to think. In the famous observation of René Descartes: *Cogito, ergo sum* ('I think, therefore I am.')

As our mind develops its capacity to think, it also develops its ability to absorb the thoughts and ideas of others. That's how it learns. Our thoughts become 'conditioned' by what we are told, what we see, hear, choose to understand and accept. It does not matter whether it is true or untrue (our subconscious mind cannot tell the difference). We develop expectations, beliefs and experiences that are stored in our subconscious mind for future reference.

They also feed our ego and determine our perception of ourselves and of everything else that exists in our world.

However, these perceptions are not reality. They are only our very limited idea of who we think we are or what we think the world is. They are largely illusions. They are the imaginings of our mind, based on what our subconscious mind or ego is telling us. And when we associate ourselves with these illusions and start to believe our own story (or the story that others tell about us) we are deluding ourselves even more! Sometimes we realize this—at least dimly—when a belief that we have held dearly is shattered by actual events and experiences. But then, all too frequently, we put the event down to fate or bad luck, or blame someone else, rather than accept that we were the cause of the problem in the first place. We will 'blame' the 'outside' world, rather than realize that the outside world is a direct reflection of our inner being.

The principle of correspondence is a very useful tool for us. It is a powerful enabling principle that allows us to see what is unknown or invisible in our current state. It enables this precisely because everything is interrelated on every plane, and so by observing what is happening on different levels we gain valuable information. If we examine carefully what is happening 'externally' as well as 'internally', we will begin to unravel the mystery of why everything is the way it is. From there, we can decide what we wish to do about it.

> This Principe is of universal application and manifestation, on the various planes of the material, mental, and spiritual universe—it is an Universal Law. The ancient Hermetists

> considered this Principle as one of the most important mental instruments by which man was able to pry aside the obstacles which hid from view the Unknown. Its use even tore aside the Veil of Isis to the extent that a glimpse of the face of the goddess might be caught.
>
> —*The Kybalion*

In order to 'pry aside the obstacles' to our learning and start to know the unknown, we need to take a calm, careful, hard look at what is happening in our external world. The outside world reflects what is happening in our inner world and will provide many useful pointers.

Then we can look more carefully at our internal world: how our physical self reflects our mental state; who we really are; what our beliefs are; where they truly came from; and how valid they are. And we can decide what to do about everything we discover. We can use this principle to unlock the door to a much better and more *enlightened* life.

How should we begin? The Ancient Greek aphorism 'Know thyself' was inscribed in the forecourt of the temple of Apollo at Delphi, where devotees went to hear about their fate from the oracle. And Socrates developed this further with his famous saying: 'An unexamined life is not worth living.'

If, then, we are to use the principle of correspondence to improve our life (as well as the lives of those around us and the condition of our world), we have to examine carefully how our life is being lived, why, and who this means we truly are.

We need to understand that what we *call* 'our life' is really the *story* of our life, which is part of who we are but only a part.

The story of our life comprises the events that have populated and populate our life at the physical and mental levels. But it is not who we are in our *essence*. It is not what we are as a human *being*. That can only be discovered at the deeper, spiritual level.

We are our life as a whole and our life is lived on three planes—physical, mental *and* spiritual. Unless we discover what this means, the principle of correspondence can only help us to a limited extent. If we perceive only the known and not the unknown, we will miss who we *are*. And who we are, which is a fundamental aspect of the principle of correspondence and of all the principles, is part of the unknown. However, let us start with discovering the *known*. In order to examine the known properly, we focus our attention on our external world—the world we inhabit that we can experience with our five basic senses.

If the reality of our external world is that we live a chaotic life, with unsatisfactory relationships and friends, and feel unfulfilled, this is a mirror of what is actually going on inside us. The same is true if we have a belief that we can have little influence on an inimical world. The thoughts inside us have manifested in our external reality. They are a powerful energetic force created on the inside that seeks expression on the outside—both in our body and on our environment. They provide a connection between the physical and non-physical dimension.

When we feel uncomfortable or unhappy on the inside (in our own body) this is a direct reflection of some negative thoughts in our conscious mind that have impressed themselves on our subconscious mind and find an energetic response in our physical body. This manifests in different ways: our body language; our tone of voice; our attitude; the language we use; even our health. All are a direct vibrational and energetic response to the vibrations sent from our mental state.

Energy flows where attention goes.

When we are negatively disposed our body language reflects the low-vibrational signals it is receiving. We look sad, our shoulders stooped. Our face shows signs of stress. And our environment senses these vibrations: the atmosphere 'darkens' and the negative energy is reflected in people's attitude towards us.

Similarly, when we are positively disposed, confident and happy, the light-vibrational energy we exude is reflected in our body and environment. We stand upright, shoulders back, smiling. We emanate an air of lightness, joy and enthusiasm. Our positive presence uplifts those around us and is reflected in the way people respond to us and treat us.

If we suffer from low self-esteem (either because we *believe* we are not good enough or *fear* that we are not good enough) or we feel bad or angry about our external environment, we will attract people and situations that correspond to and feed those beliefs. We will attract people who complain, who blame others and are never satisfied. Those who feel unworthy, are generally unhappy and talk negatively about others.

Our external world is a projection of our internal reality. Chaos in our external environment means chaos in our inner life. Negativity towards our external world is negativity in our attitude to life. Believing the worst about our external environment is believing the worst about ourselves. Seeing the world as a loveless place means an inability on our part to show love to others and to ourselves.

> If you do not have the capacity to love yourself, then there is simply no basis on which to build a sense of caring towards others. Without inner peace, it is impossible to have world peace.
>
> —Dalai Lama

Not trusting others means we do not feel wholly trustworthy ourselves. Not thanking others or showing gratitude for what we have means not recognizing the essential goodness of our own spiritual being or the beauty and love of the Universe.

These sentiments are self-perpetuating: the worse our outside world appears to us, the worse we feel about ourselves; and the worse our internal perception of ourselves, the worse the outside world. When an obese person says, 'I eat because I'm unhappy,' they are also saying, 'I'm unhappy because I eat.' Until the internal mindset changes, the negativity of the perception will prevail. The result will be self-perpetuating.

> When you hate what you are doing, complain about your surroundings, curse things that are happening or have happened, or when your internal dialogue consists of should and shouldn'ts, of blaming and accusing, then you are arguing with what *is*, arguing with that which is always already the case. You are making Life into an enemy and Life says, 'War is what you want, and war is what you get.' External reality, which always reflects back to you your inner state, is then experienced as hostile.
>
> —Eckhart Tolle, *A New Earth*

The principle of correspondence allows us to discover the reality of our internal situation by examining the outcome of our behaviours and actions as manifested in our external situation. We reap what we sow, so examining the crop provides an insight into what we have sown.

The wonderful magic of the principle of correspondence is that it enables us to make any change we want. Our thoughts, beliefs and habits are all mental constructs. As we have previously stated, they are just ideas. They are products of our imagination based on our previous experience. They are just perceptions and are not *real* unless we choose to make them so. Yet they are the basis of our external world, which reflects back to us our innermost beliefs.

Nothing in our external life can change unless we change the inside first. If we try to change the outside first, we will fail—because the outside reflects the inside. The outside is the *effect* of a *cause* we ourselves have set in motion.

When we change our internal perspective on life, alter our perceptions of who we are and, thus, change our behaviour, our external world changes too.

We have total control and power over just one area of our life: how we think, choices we make and the actions we then take.

> And there were always choices to make. Every day, every hour, offered the opportunity to make a decision, a decision whether you would or would not submit to those powers which threatened to rob you of your very self, your inner freedom; which determined whether or not you would become the plaything of circumstance, renouncing

> freedom and dignity to become moulded into the form of the typical inmate.
>
> —Viktor Frankl, *Man's Search for Meaning*

By taking control over our minds and the way we choose to perceive our world, we take control over every aspect of our life. We need to understand that this control and power can only be exercised *now*—at this very moment. It cannot be retrofitted—the past has been and gone—and it cannot be postponed into the future—which does not exist, since all future events can only be lived in the present moment.

How do we change our mindset? With the benefit of the knowledge gleaned from our analysis of our external world, we have a head start about what internal thoughts and thought processes might be creating the external events we wish to change. We need to consider carefully *how* our inner thoughts are being reflected in our external world.

For example, if we feel stress driving on a motorway because the middle lane is being 'hogged' by 'inconsiderate' drivers, we are allowing our thoughts and perception of these other drivers to dictate how we feel. We are handing over our power to people we do not know. They bear no malice towards us and are probably doing what we have done ourselves on occasion. (Even if it isn't hogging the middle lane, we certainly have other poor driving habits!) But, worse, we are allowing our perception to create unnecessary stress in our lives. This is likely to make us bad-tempered, less friendly and more prone to taking it out on others. It affects the people around us and our universe.

This is all because of a thought in our mind that we can change—should we wish to do so. It is all too often the case that the behaviours that trigger negative responses in ourselves are really only suppressed behaviours that we have not accepted or taken responsibility for.

In this example of the middle-lane hog, we are allowing ourselves to judge the actions of another person in order for our ego to feel superior. But because we cannot correct the actions of the other, we also feel unempowered and stressed. This can then escalate into anger or worse. If we do manage to solicit a response from the other driver and they move across, we will feel a brief moment of pleasure because we feel our ego has 'won'. However, a few minutes later, we find something else to criticize in another driver.

We have not resolved the issue because we have not changed anything inside of us. To resolve this stress, we have to change *our* mindset and suppress our ego by living in the moment. We have to let go of any thoughts that are negatively tinged or judgmental when we drive.

We can try repeating the words 'Let it go,' because our negative judgmental attitude absolutely doesn't serve us. Or we can repeat the phrase 'It doesn't matter,' until we believe it.

> 'The secret of change is to focus all your energy, not on fighting the old but on building the new.'
>
> —Dan Millman, *Way Of The Peaceful Warrior*

Making change happen requires a process to ensure it is durable. Having analysed our circumstances and accepted responsibility for them, we need to make a list of what it is we wish to change. We then decide what in ourselves we need to address in order to achieve the result we seek.

For example, if we come to the realization that our relationships with others are not all they should be, we should openly and humbly ask the question 'Why?' Why is it that we have few friends or we cannot keep them? Or why don't our friends seem to be very good friends? Maybe we have such a low image of ourselves that we are attracting people who reflect our poor self-esteem back to us. If we think we are surrounded by unhappy, negative and unkind friends, what makes us think that we are not exactly the same, unhappy and negative? Are we not also rather poor-quality friends?

When we judge another person, we do not define him or her, we define ourselves. Our judgment says very little of value about that other person. It only makes clear our *need* to judge that person in the way we are doing it. And in this we are saying more about ourselves than the other person.

Remember the Law of Attraction as well as this principle of correspondence. We attract what we put out. If we express low, negative vibrations, that is what we will attract back. We cannot expect to attract happy, positive friends, if we spend our time complaining, speaking negatively of others or forgetting to smile! This is obvious, but the reality is that unless we take the trouble to examine ourselves carefully, we may not even be aware that we are poor listeners, egoistic, selfish or dismissive.

Being aware of the life we are living and its impact on others is a first step to understanding what we need to change on the inside. This is not a comfortable exercise, but it is a necessary start point. We need to be clear what we want to change and be determined to do so.

Once we have established this information, in all honesty and humility, we need to make any changes we want permanent. This means creating new habits and reconditioning our subconscious so that these new behaviours become second nature.

We need to write down our new habits in the present tense and in the affirmative—as if we were like this now. For example: 'I am kind to others;' 'I let others speak first;' 'I respect the opinions of others even if I have a different perspective;' 'I smile;' 'I accept life as it is;' 'I pause for three seconds before I say anything;' 'I am comfortable with myself;' 'I am confident;' 'I love the world around me;' 'I love nature;' 'I am grateful for what I have;' 'I look at my positive statements three times a day;' 'I observe my thoughts and know how to control them;' 'I am a reliable friend;' 'I let go what I cannot do anything about;' 'I accept others for who they are.' This is the new *me*!

Remember the words in Mark 11:24, which we have highlighted before: 'What things soever ye desire, when ye pray, believe that ye receive them, and ye shall have them.'

We need to visualize the new me in all its facets and act as if it was reality right now. We need to believe that we have *already* received—not later, not when we have time, but now, in the present moment. Now is the *only time when life can be lived and change can happen.*

It may well be that others around us will not believe what they perceive. They will ask themselves, 'When will the real person we know reappear? 'When will this semblance of change fade?' And these doubts will undoubtedly also be expressed because the changes we are making are likely to be significant. If they have value, our external world will notice. This is an excellent indicator of progress.

Whether spoken or sometimes kept appropriately silent, our response is, 'Yes, that was the old me and I recognize and accept that I had to change. This is how I now wish to be. This is the new me. I am glad it is being noticed.'

In all circumstances, we need to become positively minded. We need to be can-do, 'Yes, I will' people whose 'thoughts' are those emanating from an open, not a closed, mind. We should come from a place of non-judgment rather than criticism, from a belief in independence rather than dependence, from the standpoint of acceptance rather than conflict.

We must learn to say 'Yes' to life. We have to understand that any 'No' response simply stops the flow of positive energy into ourselves and the Universe. We create our own reality through our thoughts. When we focus those thoughts on what is good, healthy, kind, loving and truthful, we come into alignment and correspondence with Oneness. We are with the light source, with Being, with universal intelligence, with unconditional love and with God. Positive thoughts with their high-quality energetic vibrations will resonate with those of other similarly minded souls and with the Universe. They will make our external world a better place. This is how the principle of correspondence can work for us and for our world. It is how we can return to harmony and the inner peace of Oneness.

Because the principle of correspondence and 'as within so without' is effective on every plane—the physical, mental and the spiritual—it means that what we think, believe and do as individuals (and collectively) will be reflected in the Universe. And what happens at the universal level will be reflected back to us.

We are all connected, that is the principle of correspondence. But it is a difficult concept to comprehend because we have been conditioned to believe only that which we can see with our own eyes or 'prove' beyond any reasonable doubt. Our education system is designed to teach us that 'mysterious' connections such as those expressed in the principle of correspondence cannot be. If anything 'special' happens, it is much easier to put this down to coincidence or a random event, than to synchronicity and universal intelligence.

Yet when we look at the subatomic, or quantum, level, we do find 'mysterious' connections. Gary Zukav explains this very well in his book on quantum physics, *The Dancing Wu Li Masters*:

> The astounding discovery awaiting newcomers to physics is that the evidence gathered in the development of quantum mechanics indicates that subatomic 'particles' constantly appear to be making decisions! More than that, the decisions they seem to make are based on decisions made elsewhere.... The philosophical implications of quantum mechanics is that all of the things in our universe, including us, that appear to exist independently are actually parts of one all-encompassing organic pattern, and that no parts of that pattern are ever really separate from it or from each other.... This means that particles are related to other particles in a systematic and intimate way that coincides with our definition of organic.

The point of explaining this connectedness and correspondence is to make clear that we are part of this system and hence connected to everything else both individually and collectively. Thus, just as we are responsible for our own individual thoughts and behaviours, we are also responsible for what happens in the world and the Universe. Both are inseparable from the whole.

This means that the state of the world is a reflection of our own thoughts, beliefs and actions. If we predominantly think negative thoughts, we not only affect ourselves, but inevitably our world.

Looking at the titles of popular newspapers and magazines, we read headlines such as: 'The Next War: The Growing Threat of Great-Power Conflict;' 'Children Taught Hatred;' and 'Heading Back to Hell: Congo in Peril.' We learn that children are watching TV programmes that invade their minds with images of so-called perfection, which they cannot attain, and which causes stress, depression, self-harm, anorexia and bulimia. Similarly, we read about the negative effects of social media. They portray images of a utopic existence that simply doesn't exist. Or show apparently magnificent celebrity occasions depicting gloriously happy people, when the truth is so very different. We read of the dysfunctional relationships of many well-known couples, of the obsession with form, things and possessions. We see the catastrophic consequences of our selfishness, ignorance and ego-generated desires, wants and fears.

If we have oceans filled with plastic particles that kill birds and fish and alter the delicate balance of the ecology, it is the direct result of our irresponsible actions. If many species of life-saving plants and animals are at risk of extinction, it is the result of our decimating our environment for the sake of having enough heat, electricity and other conveniences. We enjoy them at other species' expense—suffocating life, theirs and ours. If we have built the capacity to destroy ourselves by the push of a button, it is the result of our ability to invent new and more powerful weapons out of fear of our neighbours.

All these things are the products of our individual and collective minds. They are self-perpetuating because our negative thoughts create a negative environment and our negative environment promotes our negative thoughts. Everything is connected and corresponds to everything else.

As human beings we have a responsibility to change this and the ability to do so. Because we are the very source of thought (through our connection to divine intelligence) we have immense power and can change whatever we put our minds to.

Several practices give us the strength to work with universal and divine intelligence: our willingness to say 'Yes'; promoting positive thoughts and actions instead of negative ones; being courageous in our beliefs; and educating our children to the power of positivity, the beauty of Oneness and the creation of hope. These give us the determination to make collective choices that will transform the understanding and consciousness of the human species—before it is too late.

We are One, we are connected. We are not separate. We are not divided. Oneness is the very essence of reality. We have the choice to either change the thoughts, beliefs and behaviours of the human race. Otherwise, humanity will destroy itself and its beautiful world. We have to make changes that will doubtless affect our lifestyle, our comforts and our possessions. We will maybe have to reduce some of the luxuries we enjoy. However, the consequences of not doing so are cataclysmic—as we all, in our heart of hearts, know only too well.

We need leaders who realize that we cannot stay divided and separate. They have to understand that we need to think at a higher, more enlightened and altruistic level. And they should, with dignity and humility, seek peaceful, awakened, conscious solutions rather than short-term, self-seeking and selfishly motivated hits. We need leaders in all walks of life who are committed to working in harmony and understanding—for the benefit of all mankind, not just the few.

And we, every one of us, need to take full responsibility to do all we can to help everyone see the light, to awaken to a new reality, to become conscious of who we really are. We are the children of God, created in the image of God. In the words of Jesus: 'For, behold, the kingdom of God is within you' (Luke 17:21).

> No one saves us but ourselves.
> No one can and no one may.
> We ourselves must walk the path.
>
> —The Dhammapada
> (rendered by Paul Carus)

We need to educate every human being to this knowledge of connectedness, correspondence, Oneness, positivity, respect, ego control and the guiding principles of the golden rule. We need to encourage voters to vote not for those who shout loudest in support of their particular self-interest and divisive ideology, but for those who support a fairer, more compassionate, more humane, safer, cleaner and more loving world. We need a world in which our children and our children's children can live in peace and harmony.

17

Gender—Our Feminine and Masculine Traits

Have you ever wondered whether it is inevitable that men should be 'from Mars' and women 'from Venus' and that the two genders should have such differing and separate characteristics?

Have you considered whether the question of gender is just about 'men' and 'women' and their physical difference or are there characteristics of both genders that exist in males *and* females and need to be balanced?

Do you believe it to be true that men are predominantly 'left-brained' and 'logical' whereas women are more 'right brained' and 'intuitive'?

Have you ever questioned the gender of God who is often pictured as a man with a flowing beard? Is this masculine image compatible with the concept of universal intelligence, eternal light and divine creator, all of which have no gender?

Do you sometimes wonder whether the issues and conflicts of our time are in any way related to the imbalance between male and female traits in our society?

> Gender is in everything: everything has its masculine and feminine principles; Gender manifests on all planes.
>
> —*The Kybalion*

Everything in our universe and all creation is the result of masculine and feminine bonding and this applies at all the levels—physical, mental and spiritual.

It manifests in physical things, including the generation of electrons, protons and atoms. It is evident in plants, which require both male and female energies to co-create, just as it applies to human beings, who all display various degrees of masculine and feminine principles within them.

It shows up on the mental plane—in thoughts, situations and events—where the balance or imbalance between the masculine and the feminine have significant effects.

It is also present on the spiritual plane: the outcome of a state of perfect balance achieved between the yin and the yang results in the human being finding complete alignment with Oneness.

This Oneness, which can also be referred to as the superconscious mind, comprises both the masculine and feminine elements in such harmony that it reflects *both and neither* at the same time. Oneness represents the ultimate combination of male and female in perfect balance. At this point, it ceases to be dual and lies above any differences found on the physical and mental planes.

The path to inner peace, therefore, is when the male and female aspects within the self are perfectly balanced and mirror the state of Oneness, which is the ultimate goal. In the words of the Hermetic philosophy: 'All souls are parts of one Soul, which is the Soul of the Cosmos. Souls all have one nature. They are neither male or female. Such differences of gender arise only in the body.'

Gender is evident and present in everything and is always at work. Nothing can be created without both male and female energies. Understanding how this operates at different levels opens up an interesting perspective on almost every subject and situation.

Although often described as male and female (and sometimes also as positive and negative energetic charges) these energies might more accurately be described as masculine and feminine to avoid the impression that there is anything negative about either. They are purely descriptions. They are not directly related to sexual gender since they apply to both men and women. As with most concepts and ideas, they are neither 'good' nor 'bad' but just *are*. They are neutral in the sense that they simply need to be understood and then applied by us in the best way possible to achieve the greatest good.

This concept is primarily about creation and generation. The word 'gender' has its roots in both Latin—*genus*, meaning 'type' or 'sort'—and Greek—*gen*, meaning 'to produce', as in oxygen, which is that which produces oxy (acid). On the physical level, gender is about procreation: the bonding of the masculine and feminine elements creates the next generation and perpetuates the species. This applies to plants and animals, as well as things, such as electricity, magnetism, cells and protons, where a negative and a positive charge combine to create new substances and new life.

Everything and everyone contain the two elements *within* him or her. Every female thing contains the masculine element and every male thing contains the feminine element. It is the degree to which they are present and in *balance* that matters. Imbalances result in dis-harmony and dysfunctionality. This makes it similar to the concept of polarity: the masculine and feminine elements are at each pole, yet, in this case, they need to combine together for creation and find balance for harmony.

The masculine characteristics are externally directed, straight, square, consistent, loyal, disciplined, analytical, logical ('left brained'), action-oriented, active, forceful, assertive, canine, dynamic and provide will and determination. In electromagnetism, it is the magnetic side and the plus sign on a battery. This is the positive polarity. This is yang.

The feminine characteristics are internally directed, curved, round, creative, accepting, passive, feline, desiring, emotive, spontaneous, intuitive, empathetic, imaginative, restful, caring, inward-flowing, compassionate, collaborative and receiving. In electromagnetism, it is the electrical side, the minus sign on a battery. This is the negative polarity. This is yin.

The masculine energy pushes outside of itself, penetrates and provides the blueprint. While the feminine energy attracts into itself and assimilates the blueprint in order to create and give birth.

On the mental plane, thoughts and emotions (emotion = energy in motion) will have a combination of masculine and feminine factors. If there is a preponderance of masculine factors, the thoughts and emotions will be primarily direct, logical, theoretical, linear, action oriented and forceful. Where there is a preponderance of feminine elements, the thoughts and emotions will be primarily gentle, intuitive, creative, circumspect, collaborative and nurturing.

When our spiritual awareness generates creative ideas, thoughts and concepts, this is the product of the feminine element within us. It will only produce results, however, when combined with the action-orientated will of the masculine element within us.

Sounds only convert into music when beat, a masculine element, is combined with melody, a feminine element.

At the atomic level, masculine protons seek feminine electrons, which are attracted to these masculine protons. Under the impulse of masculine energy, the feminine particles vibrate rapidly and circle at great speed around the proton. The creative process is launched, and a new atom is created. This union of protons and electrons is responsible for the existence of magnetism, electricity, heat, light, attraction and repulsion. It is in constant operation in the fields of matter and energy, as it is on every plane.

The reason why this concept is of such importance is that the balance between masculine and feminine elements is reflected in every aspect of our life and world. It enables us to examine carefully—and from a different perspective—how balanced we are as individuals, as a society and as a world. We can see the extent to which that balance is aligned and in spiritual balance with Oneness and universal intelligence.

When we are out of balance (as individuals or as a society) we become dysfunctional. We can be either too aggressive or too passive, too intimidating or too submissive, too domineering and power seeking or too timid and withdrawn. At either extreme, the results are often catastrophic. This imbalance is revealed in our personal relationships, as well as the conflicts within societal groups and between nations.

At the individual and personal level, we have to examine our own thoughts. As Socrates taught, and we have quoted several times, 'The unexamined life is not worth living.' It is by taking a hard look at our own comportment that we will learn about our self and how we can improve. We have to become the honest, truthful and impartial *observers of our thoughts* (as individuals and collectively) to assess to what extent we as individuals and our society as a whole are in balance.

Are our habits, attitudes and behaviours predominantly masculine or feminine? And to what extent and with what implications?

To what extent do we display each of them in our daily life in the way we respond to events and circumstances? Are we forceful, action and achievement oriented and analytical, but not given to bringing other people along with us? Or are we more intuitive, creative, imaginative, considerate and caring but perhaps less concerned with results?

This is the domain of psychology in all its forms. There have been extensive studies on and around this subject, including in-depth psychographic studies, NLP (neuro linguistic programming) and many more. Nevertheless, there is great value in us just *looking* at our own actions, reactions and behaviour under various conditions. We should judge our own conduct against normative balanced criteria in order to obtain a reasonable sense of how balanced we are.

Against any given situation, we can analyse our attitude and reactions to determine whether we have a bias towards masculine or feminine traits. An honest conversation with a good friend or family member will also be very accurate and useful— as long as we are willing to listen!

Another way of understanding more about our self is to take a look at the results we are achieving. These will always be a reflection and consequence of our inner thoughts and the balance we have.

For example, do we enjoy harmonious relationships of confidence, love and trust with our partner and family, while also leading a productive life, achieving practical results and having a wide range of interests? Or are our relationships generally rather fractious, with frequent crises in which we feel misunderstood and unloved? Do we have a few good friends on whom we can depend, whose company we enjoy and who accept us for who we are, just as we accept them for who they are? Or do we have many superficial friends who come and go and who we would prefer to keep at arm's length? Do we enjoy our work and what we do, find we have appropriate influence, feel respected, engaged and enthusiastic? Or do we find our job burdensome, where we have little impact, we feel put upon, stressed and unempowered and where we feel we have a particularly difficult boss?

Do we live a generally happy life, with plentiful laughter, a sense of fun and *joie de vivre* and a feeling of awe at the beauty of our world in all its many and varied manifestations? Or do we wake up in the morning bemoaning life's regrettable accidents, our lack of good fortune, the rude nature of our increasingly difficult world, the harried and hurried life we live and the poor prospects of the future?

The world we have created for our self says everything about who we are. And if we want to change our world, we have to change our self. Trying to change our world by focusing on the outside can never work because the outside is just a reflection of our inner thoughts. It is like trying to improve the image in the mirror by drawing on it!

Another way to discover who we are is to consider which particular behaviours we are *least happy* to adopt.

For example, if we like to be in the limelight and find it more uncomfortable taking a back seat, we need to learn the value of modesty and humility. We could not only invite others to take charge but also allow them to do so!

If we tend to prefer doing the talking and find it hard not to intervene, we need to learn the wisdom of silence. In this case, we could develop the habit of never speaking first.

If we prefer to be the generator of new ideas and are creatively open to all things but find it hard to complete projects, then we need to learn to focus more. We should undertake fewer activities at the same time and set clear goals.

If we find we tend to avoid conflict and, as a result, reluctantly accept decisions made by others with which we are not in agreement, we need to learn to be more assertive and self-confident.

If we find it difficult to listen to the opinions of people who have different views from our own and tend to go away feeling misunderstood, then we need to learn to be more receptive and respectful of others. We have to recognize that, in reality, we know very little. As Socrates said, 'I know that I know nothing!' The more we 'know', the more we realize how little we truly know.

In almost all societies across the world, boys and men have been encouraged and conditioned to believe that they should be forceful, direct, analytical, problem-solving, results-oriented and, as a result, dominant.

Similarly, girls and women have been encouraged and conditioned to be receptive, nurturing, accepting and gentle but, also, weak (as in the phrase 'the weaker sex'!) and subservient.

This conditioning, perpetuated throughout the centuries, is in direct opposition and contrary to natural law, harmony, respect for human beings and Oneness.

What is worse is that, in the process, the essential feminine traits have been suppressed in both men and women. The result is that we ourselves (as well as our societies) are severely out of balance. We tend towards a clear and definitive masculine bias. This is evidenced by the value placed on winning, on being right, on conquering, on 'succeeding' at all costs. There is no regard of the consequences, however horrendous, to our families, children and neighbours. Nor to our health, environment, world, to life itself.

The extreme degree to which the world has been biased towards masculine traits can be demonstrated by the very significant number of imbalances and inequalities that clearly remain. (And this in spite of very considerable and selfless efforts by many to rectify this.) This can be seen at the physical level such as the still current practice of female genital mutilation, the actual murder of female children, as well as the inability of women to progress in the workplace, have their own possessions, be seen in public or sit in the same locations or at the same tables as men. Everything external here reflects an internal dialogue. In this case, the belief developed over many centuries that men are somehow better, should be in charge and in control. This is part of the general attitude that has denigrated the feminine side of human beings.

The obsession with left-brain, analytical, logical, science-based consciousness coupled with the apparent encouragement to be forceful, direct and opinionated has resulted in a world that has become ever more aggressive, divided and dangerous. This is despite the fact we live in a time when the complexities we face require much deeper thought, creativity and compassion.

Our education system places considerable focus on the more masculine traits of facts and figures, mathematics and science. This is at the expense of the more feminine traits of music, art, interpersonal skills and communication, gentleness and creativity—let alone teaching how to live harmoniously, in peace, respecting all others with tolerance and humility.

The so-called softer skills, more essential today than ever before, are not taught in school. Nor are there courses on how we need to live with a different way of thinking. Parents also have a major role to play in helping their children develop both their masculine and feminine sides—to enable them to grow up with a balanced perspective.

Albert Einstein recognized this need to think differently and with a better balance throughout his life. He was a deep thinker and philosopher as well as a brilliant scientist. The way he was generally portrayed as a brilliant scientist irritated him because he wanted the world to know that his scientific insights were not simply the result of his scientific analytical abilities (essentially masculine traits) but much more the product of his intuition, imagination and creativity (feminine traits).

> Imagination is more important than knowledge. For knowledge is limited to all we now know and understand, while imagination embraces the entire world.
>
> —Albert Einstein, interview (1929)

Both sides of his brain and both the masculine and feminine sides of his character were in operation. They worked together in order for him to arrive at his insights. It is his insights that gave birth to his scientific brilliance.

With the splitting of the atom, Albert Einstein clearly understood that human beings were on a course of utter destruction and annihilation unless a new way of thinking could be adopted. The divisive, conflict-ridden, masculine dominated ways that had existed for at least the previous two and a half thousand years needed to change and change rapidly in order to catch up with the speed of scientific 'progress'.

And this understanding was encapsulated by Ram Dass (whom we quoted earlier): 'Einstein said an interesting thing, "The world that we have made as a result of the level of thinking we have done thus far creates problems that we cannot solve at the same level as the level we created them at."'

During the past century, there has been remarkable progress in rebalancing masculine and feminine traits in ourselves and in many of our societies. It has been enlightening and encouraging to witness the extent to which younger generations have rejected previous practices and embraced this rebalance. They manifest it naturally in their daily lives and it is supported by more emancipated legal regulation. It is to be hoped that they will continue to uphold these values—even in the face of determined opposition.

This bodes well for our need to move from separateness to Oneness, from intolerance and division to acceptance and togetherness and from conflict to collaboration. It is a move from negativity to positivity. We no longer see the world as a dangerous, inimical place but as a place of peace and possibility. It's the passage from hate to love, from violence to peace.

Many luminaries of our recent past, such as Mahatma Gandhi, Martin Luther King, Nelson Mandela and Robert Kennedy, as well as the many others who are less well known or unknown, stood for these values and often died for them. They sought to change the way we and society think in order to create a new and better world.

We need to continue to change the way we think and our internal world, so that we attract and create the external world we want. We need to ignore the bombardment of negative messages to which we are subjected every day. We need to talk about, think about and absorb all the positive actions and possibilities that exist and happen every day.

Our education system needs to encompass this type of thinking—not as something nebulous, unverifiable and unmarkable, but as an essential part of creating a peaceful and happier world. Facts and figures, logic and theory, however worthy, are no substitute for what really matters in life: peace and harmony, kindness and compassion, respect and love of others and the avoidance of judgment and opinion.

> 'Whatsoever ye would that men should do to you, do ye even so unto them: for this is the law and the prophets.'
>
> —Matthew 7:12

> 'Judge not that ye be not judged. For with what judgment ye judge, ye shall be judged.'
>
> —Matthew 7:1

If we think negative thoughts, then that is the world we will inhabit. The same is true if we think with our left brain and with predominantly masculine characteristics. Or if we spend our time judging others and sowing the seeds of discord.

When we look at the history of mankind, it is largely about division and war, self-inflicted suffering and violence. It is about differences. The masculine trait has driven progress and winning. It's about being right and the other (person, group, religion, race, gender, belief) wrong. We create fear and foment hate by emphasizing difference rather than similarity. And this is also true when we deliberately ignore or severely restrict the importance of the feminine traits of cooperation, tolerance, acceptance and compassion.

Seen objectively (as someone from another planet coming to observe us and our history might), our history and behaviour pattern could be described as collective criminal insanity. We have been chronically and pathological paranoid in our behaviour pattern—destroying our neighbours, our environment, ourselves and our beautiful world seemingly indiscriminately—and for reasons that make no sense in the context of Oneness. The world cannot survive if we continue with this type of thinking.

While there have been magnificent, extraordinary and astonishingly beautiful achievements in the arts, technology, medicine and every other field of human endeavour, the accompanying unconscious, ego-based insanity has resulted in the development of a scientific and technological capability of unprecedented self-destruction.

> I believe there will always be wars, until perchance we all become so spiritual that by the evolution of our individual natures we will make war unnecessary. No matter what their differences, if great minds such as Jesus, Krishna, Buddha, Mohammed, sat together, they would never use the engines of science to try to destroy each other. Why must people feel it necessary to fight? The power of guns evokes no wisdom, nor has it ever accomplished lasting peace.
>
> —Paramahansa Yogananda

In conclusion, there is a great need to balance or rebalance the masculine and feminine sides of our being (individually and collectively) and establish a new way of thinking that is not based on separation but on unity. It has to be based on the recognition that—as we have indicated throughout this book—we are all part of one Universe, one perfect Heaven, one cosmic energetic force from which we came and to which we will return. We have to free ourselves from a divisive mode of thinking—ego-based, negative and restricting—in order to break out of the prison we have created for ourselves.

> A human being is a part of the whole called by us 'Universe', a part limited in time and space. He experiences himself, his thoughts and feelings, as something separated from the rest, a kind of optical delusion of his consciousness....
>
> This delusion is a kind of prison for us, restricting us to our personal desires and to affection for a few persons nearest to us. Our task must be to free ourselves from this prison by widening our circle of compassion to embrace all living creatures and the whole of nature in its beauty.
>
> —Albert Einstein, two letters on death (1950)

There is a little known, but highly significant, event that took place in October 1962, at the height of the Cuban Missile Crisis. Soviet ships had been sent by Moscow to deliver nuclear ballistic missiles to Fidel Castro's Cuba, but were blocked by US warships and a stalemate ensued. Both nations were ready to unleash a nuclear war in defence of their position.

On 27 October, the US navy discovered a nuclear-armed Soviet submarine, B-59, near Cuba and dropped depth charges that forced the submarine to dive very deep, where communications with the outside world were not possible. The crew and their leadership were thus unaware of the state of the crisis or whether a nuclear war had already begun.

The captain of the submarine decided categorically that a war had probably started and opted to launch a nuclear torpedo. His decision was supported by the political officer on board. Only the flotilla commander, Vasili Arkhipov, adamantly held out on a decision that was required to be unanimous. No nuclear weapon was launched. This was described by the John F Kennedy administration as 'not only the most dangerous moment of the Cold War. It was the most dangerous moment in human history.'

Vasili Arkhipov rarely spoke about the event afterwards. Here was a career soldier, disciplined and trained to fight and win (essentially masculine traits) who showed courage in maintaining his position and displaying the feminine traits of compassion and respect for humanity.

The Future of Life Institute (FLI) recognized this act of bravery as an example of how human beings of integrity and in positions of power can, should and must prevent technology from destroying the world. This event is a salutary warning and needs to be heeded with even more intensity today.

PART 3

The Way *to* Change How We Think To Save Our Future

18

The Issues We Face

In Parts 1 and 2, we considered some of the issues facing mankind and many of the reasons for our continuing conflict-ridden world. Regrettably, the evolution of our consciousness has not kept pace with the evolution of our capacity to think. We have created a very 'left-brained' culture in which logic, evidence, scientific 'proof', facts and figures are given much greater prominence and authority than intuition, creativity, imagination, wisdom and diplomacy. Cold data holds more sway than intuitive wisdom—even when the data and the facts are subsequently shown to be erroneous or incomplete and have caused a domino effect that was never anticipated. We then blame the algorithm. *It* must have been at fault, not the logic of the mind behind it that, however brilliant, failed to recognize the wider implications.

In spite of many significant and successful attempts to make changes to society and its practices, we still have a very 'masculine' perspective. Forcefulness, ostentation, bravado, aggression and the accumulation of wealth are seen as of more value and as positive visible symbols of 'success' than quiet common sense, gentleness, decency, consideration for others and humility. Voters appear to be more attracted to loud rants and clever soundbites than expressions of considered wisdom.

At a time when the world should be seeking global solutions to global issues and collaboration instead of conflict, the demands of population growth and selfish aspirations mean that, while some inequalities have reduced, there remain appalling and obscene disparities. Look at factors such as children's mortality rates, education, wealth, nourishment and health—between and within countries as well as continents.

We are living in a highly dangerous world. Technological and scientific advances in military, medical and IT capabilities (AI, cyber warfare, privacy) make the risk of a catastrophic event (whether by accident or deliberate design) both easier and more probable. The potential for disaster today is on an unimaginable scale, which is why many scientists are pessimistic about the prospects for humanity. They realize—as Einstein did on discovering his theory of relativity that foreshadowed the development of the atomic bomb—that we face annihilation unless we seriously change the way we think.

All technological advances have potential for good and the manifestation of this is hugely evident in every aspect of our life. But if they are misused by unscrupulous and controlling individuals (or states) for the purpose of gaining power or control over others, they have the equal potential for bad. At a time of great uncertainty and changes to the previous relative balance of peace between nations, the risk of war between countries has increased, as the geopolitical tectonic plates shift.

We also face environmental dangers associated with an increasingly unstable physical world—a direct consequence of our desire for ever greater comforts, convenience, protein, leisure, cheap goods, and so on. The issue of climate change and environmental destruction has been well documented, but the effects are only just beginning to happen. Droughts, storms, floods, insufficient and inadequate drinking water, fires, extremes of heat and cold, desertification, deforestation, melting ice caps and glaciers, polluted oceans, rising water levels, the extinction of animal and insect species are just some of the challenges humanity faces. We have unleashed a series of actions, many of which are unstoppable. All we will be able to do is face them and their consequences, which include deep political and social implications.

We are also subjected to a constant barrage of negative news in the media. We are shown violence and random acts of killing and shooting. Similarly, TV and internet programmes contain graphic images of extreme hate and cruelty, and we are encouraged to play addictive, bloodthirsty computer and internet games. Even well-intentioned entertainment is often toxic to the mind of young people. It projects unrealistic and dangerous images of health, wealth and beauty with which young people are encouraged to compare themselves. Or it shows everyday scenes of family violence, obscene behaviour and language, which makes this 'acceptable' behaviour and a terrible example to our children.

Where are the role models for the young to follow?

Parents often ignore their children. They prefer to watch films or play computer games rather than engage in conversation, which would provide the foundation of deep and loving relationships. These essential building blocks of trust and compassion are vital, not least when real problems surface—which they inevitably will. Parents are the first and most important role models that children have. It is a very great responsibility that cannot be taken lightly.

Education is no longer fit for purpose. It focuses on performance tables relying on verifiable quantitative measurements, facts and figures, crammed into the young, rather than the less measurable but more important qualities of creativity, collaboration, emotional development, altruism and awareness.

Our institutions, whether private, public, charitable or religious are creaking and there is considerable scepticism and lack of trust in them. Even though significant positive changes are occurring—not least in big corporations who, in many respects, are leading the way—almost all our institutions are viewed with great suspicion. Corporations are perceived as only interested in profit not people. While other organisations are considered self-serving, corrupt or incompetent. This is hardly surprising given the scandals, catastrophic and often unpunished mistakes, obscene greed and selfishness of executives and those in authority.

Where are the role models for the young to follow?

There is, above all, a crisis of leadership. The perception, here too, is of arrogance, incompetence and greed. There is an absence of statesmanship and a total disregard of the greater good, let alone the future of the planet. Many of the world's most powerful countries and their leaders are fuelling a spirit of nationalism and divisiveness. They have created polarised societies where the possibility of compromise has diminished. They engage in an arms race and the demonstration of force rather than a search for peace.

The world's greatest issues are increasingly complex. They require careful and proper understanding, planning and patience. They require competence and courage, humility and compassion. Many solutions require a global, not parochial, perspective. They cannot be solved by a single country on its own. They require humility in accepting that solutions are not easy and will take time, patience and collaboration.

Where are the statesmen and women, the peacemakers, the wise leaders, the calm voices of common sense?

Or can such people never be elected by an electorate clamouring for clever soundbites and a charismatic image?

Where are the leaders described by Lao Tzu in the Tao Te Ching, verse 17 (rendered by Stephen Mitchell), in this way?

> When the Master governs, the people
> are hardly aware that he exists.
> Next best is a leader who is loved.
> Next, one who is feared.
> The worst is one who is despised.
>
> If you don't trust the people,
> you can make them untrustworthy.
>
> The Master doesn't talk, he acts.
> When his work is done, the people say. 'Amazing:
> we did it, all by ourselves!'

Or again, in verse 66:

> All streams flow to the sea
> because it is lower than they are.
> Humility gives it its power.
>
> If you want to govern the people
> you must place yourself below them.
> If you want to lead the people,
> you must learn how to follow them.

19

What Solutions Can We Propose? The Individual Level

Given the issues we have enumerated and their scale, it would be very presumptuous to suggest that we have a magic wand that can make everything right. We don't. All we have is the wisdom of the sages of the past, their teachings, their guidance and their experience. Much of it dates back many hundreds, even thousands, of years. We also have the wisdom of those enlightened individuals throughout history who have achieved miraculous outcomes despite—and sometimes because of—the enormity of the problems they faced.

Is this knowledge still relevant today?

Humanity is in grave danger and facing extinction. The way we currently think has led us to this point. Our thinking is based on the belief that we are separate and individual. We see our role in life to better ourselves and to be 'successful'. Success is measured by the achievement of personal goals, recognition by society, positions, titles and all the trappings of wealth with the assumed 'power' that comes from these. We 'want', 'need' and 'strive' in order to have more: more things, more fame, better looks, more exotic holidays, greater wealth.

In and of itself, this is not necessarily bad. The progress of society depends on the energy and drive of people striving for goals, making new discoveries and achieving new feats. The problems begin when our wants and needs become the sole or main purpose of our life and we become attached to them.

We invest things with a sense of identity. We feel we are better than someone else because we own something. The ownership of things, wealth and opinions become primordial and overwhelming. Our attachment, which is a thought generated by our egoic mind, then takes over and *becomes who we are.* We become the thoughts of our ego.

The ego then controls everything we do: our emotions, our actions and re-actions. Once ego has taken over, it does everything it can to defend and enhance the false image it has created. Yet it can never be satisfied because it is an illusion. When it gets what it wants, it craves more. When it doesn't get what it wants, it suffers until it does. It fights, lies, cheats—whatever is needed—to satisfy its selfish desires.

Our anxieties, fears, resentments and envies, our 'needs' and 'wants' are all the product of our egoic mind. They are, in reality, just thoughts—constructs of the mind that are unreal and fleeting. But to our highly insecure ego, fanatically attached to this illusion, *these thoughts are our identity.* Any diminution or destruction of this image is viewed as an attack on our entire person. If the attack is successful, we are diminished, even to the point of feeling we have died. This is because to our ego we have died, since this identity, however delusional, is the only one the ego has. The belief in the image can be so great that when major problems occur the image is shattered and this can even lead to suicide. Ego is more interested in protecting its assumed image than in protecting the life of the real person. A slave to the impulses of his own ego, the person then prefers death to the destruction of his illusory identity. Ego never serves its host.

The news report of a recent tragedy in the UK illustrates this clearly:

> A financier and former director of a bank deliberately drowned himself in his swimming pool as he thought he was about to be investigated by the Financial Conduct Authority and sent to prison.... A millionaire who owned properties [he] had become convinced the regulator was going to send him to jail and he began to suffer from manic episodes.
>
> —*The Times*, 8 August 2019

Similarly, a 2001 survey involving 13,601 US students from ninth to twelfth grade published in *Archives of Paediatrics & Adolescent Medicine* found that:

> Suicidal impulses are much more common in teenagers who think they are too fat or too thin, regardless of how much they actually weigh. In the study, 19% said they had considered suicide the previous year and about 9% said they attempted it. About 65% of students were in the normal-weight range, but only 54% perceived themselves as being the right weight.

When ego takes over and image, identity and self-importance become the most important element of our life, we naturally become self-absorbed, greedy, aggressive and arrogant. We believe we are more 'special' than anyone else and separate from them. We are trapped in 'object' consciousness and in 'form'. In this state, we are the prisoners of our ego and have no conception of who we really are. We can never feel truly satisfied or complete. There is always something missing.

When our obsession with 'things' leads us to worry more about our possessions than the happiness of the people around us, peace and joy will always elude us.

> Fame or integrity: which is more important?
> Money or happiness: which is more valuable?
> Success or failure: which is more destructive?
>
> If you look to others for fulfilment,
> you will never truly be fulfilled.
> If your happiness depends on money,
> you will never be happy with yourself.
>
> Be content with what you have:
> rejoice in the way things are.
> When you realise there is nothing lacking,
> the whole world belongs to you.
>
> —Lao Tzu, Tao Te Ching, verse 44
> (rendered by Stephen Mitchell)

The dominance of ego, which has been the prime driving characteristic of human beings for thousands of years, is now the greatest threat to the survival of our species and our world. This was recognised by the sages of the past who warned of these consequences and pointed to a different way. Unless we overcome the power of ego to control our lives and a new dimension of consciousness emerges, humanity will disappear.

To appreciate this, all we need do is read some history, observe what is happening every day and listen to the news.

We are faced with an evident choice: evolve or die!

This is not scaremongering. Just take a look around and see for yourself. We are living on borrowed time. And we are all in it together.

We are not separate

To evolve to a new, deeper level of consciousness requires us to understand this very point: *we are not separate*, however much we sometimes like to think we are. We are part of a much greater intelligence and power. *We are all connected.* What we do affects the whole universe. Our interdependence requires us to honour the existence of all who share our planet. We need to move from object consciousness and dependence on form to spiritual consciousness and the world of the formless—beauty, joy, wisdom and love.

The role of ego and the egoic mind, which served us well as we evolved from our previous animal state, is now no longer helpful. It has become a dangerous liability and we either evolve beyond it or become extinct (the fate of all species unable to adapt).

The greatest role and purpose we now have is to raise our own consciousness beyond ego and thought and help raise the level of consciousness of humanity. We must evolve away from the selfishness of ego to a new dimension of compassion, kindness, inclusiveness and love. This new dimension is not a return to a mythical paradise that may have existed before ego appeared, but a dimension where ego is controlled and subservient to the wisdom of a consciousness that goes beyond thought and transcends ego.

While some may scoff at this and view it as weak and idealistic, we only need to observe what is happening around the world to realise that the current model is a failing one. It is leading us down the road to extinction. The evolution of our egoic mind has taken us to the brink of collapse and we live in a dysfunctional and mad world. To continue unchanged and expect a different result is madness. The way we currently operate is broken.

The solution is inside us already

The wonderful thing is that the solution is inside us—right now. We do not need to make new technological discoveries, invent new courses or go on exotic pilgrimages. We do not need to look to some future state. We simply need to remove the conditioning of our egoic mind to reveal the essence of who we are.

The answer does not lie outside of us—where the egoic mind tries in vain to find more— but inside us, at a deeper, more aware level. Awareness can only exist in the present moment, the now. Heaven is within us and is unveiled by awareness. What lies 'outside' this truth is then seen as an illusion, an appearance, a drama created by the distorted perception of our mind. Human beings are so used to living in this illusory world that anxiety, stress, fear, resentment, guilt and remorse are considered a 'normal' state of consciousness and 'real'. When we remove this distortion we learn what is truly real. It is what happens in the permanence and safety of the present moment. Then we discover that what is inside is free of all negativity and conditioning. It is a place of truth, joy, love and peace. This is our opportunity to make changes to ourselves by adopting a different way to think. We can then help others do the same.

By becoming the observers and not the servants of our ego, we remove the barriers to the essence of who we are and access a deep sense of alert peacefulness and goodness. From this place, we rediscover the beauty of life. We rediscover nature, which we had ignored when we 'had no time' because of our obsession with chasing things. We awaken to the madness of our actions, to the fact that we know not what we do. We rediscover what it is to be kind and considerate, respectful and unselfish. We rediscover what is and what is not important. We rediscover that we have a temporary, human, mortal form, which we have been given the privilege to inhabit for a short time. And we realise that we have a spiritual self, a presence that is formless.

We cannot see, touch or feel or understand this self intellectually but only experience it. Unlike our human form, which is temporal and unreal, our spiritual self is eternal and infinite. We can then live life fully without fear—even of death. We awaken from the dream (or nightmare) of our previous existence as the light of this greater truth shines in us. This awakening is the realisation that we live life in the present moment only and that the present moment is the only moment that exists—unpolluted by ego, unattached to form.

Life on earth is a gift. It is an opportunity to do good and to serve. It will be over very quickly.

The ideas we have outlined in *The Way* give many indicators of how to start the process of change and some methodology for starting the journey to discovering who we are (and have always been) at the deepest, spiritual level.

We have learnt to be the observers of our thoughts rather than believe we are our thoughts. We have learnt to be aware of our awareness, to be the space within which our thoughts and our awareness happens, to be the depths of the ocean of our Being rather than the life story that happens on its surface. We have learnt that we *are* awareness, spaciousness, presence and a microcosm of the macrocosm of universal intelligence (or whatever description we wish to use to point to this infinite power that cannot be comprehended let alone described). We have learnt to access this sacred place within ourselves through stillness and meditation, through emptying our mind of thought, through surrender to the Oneness and love.

> We join spokes together in a wheel,
> but it is the centre hole
> that makes the wagon move.
>
> We shape clay into a pot,
> but it is the emptiness inside
> that holds whatever we want.
>
> We hammer wood for a house,
> but it is the inner space that makes it livable.
>
> We work with being,
> but non-being is what we use.
>
> —Lao Tzu, Tao Te Ching, verse 11
> (rendered by Stephen Mitchell)

Our role at the individual level is to reconnect to universal intelligence. Our purpose is to make a gift of the only possession we truly have: our life. We help raise humanity and its consciousness by being kind, compassionate, tolerant, humble, forgiving and loving in all that we do. We respect nature—animals, birds, insects and the inhabitants of our oceans. This is not through an effort of willpower, but because that is *our truth*. It is our awareness and our consciousness. It is how we can make the most difference *right now*. It is how we can create peace in turbulent times and save our planet. We do not need more time. We can start immediately. We have all we need within us.

No one has a monopoly on truth

No one has a monopoly of truth. (In fact, no one can even know what truth is since the mind is not capable of *knowing*. The mind can only 'know about' things based on assumptions and perceptions.) No one has the right to consider themselves better, more spiritual, more righteous or more worthy than anyone else. That would be allowing ego to surreptitiously resurface where the opposite is sought.

At the spiritual level, there is only perfection. At the human level, there is only imperfection, which is the human condition. Life is suffering. Surrendering to suffering opens a crack in the armour, which allows the light to shine in. Humility then arises, which is the antidote to ego. With humility, the world that the ego pictures with itself at its centre is revealed as the vain illusion that it is.

The Way does not wish to suggest that it has all the answers or indeed any: it simply seeks to provide signposts to what may help individuals find a sense of peace in a complicated world. Whatever works for people is fine. If different ideas, beliefs, practices, therapies or concepts work, that's fine too. By 'work' we mean a spiritual awareness of love that results in an experience of peace, the desire to contribute positively to society, to uplift others and help them evolve spiritually. With selfless service and devotion to goodness, every smile, every gesture of kindness, every act of compassion is spiritually uplifting.

20

What Solutions Can We Propose? The Collective Level

Our prime task is to develop our understanding of who we are at the spiritual level and live life in alignment with this awareness. It is to raise our level of consciousness and help others do the same. It is about understanding the force of ego and distancing ourselves from its devastatingly negative thoughts. The challenges presented by our society can only be addressed when our collective level of consciousness is sufficiently evolved to enable this to happen. Being in alignment means acting with integrity and going beyond the falsehoods of our individual and collective ego. It means being transparent and exposing truth. It means having the courage to stand up for what is right and decent.

Like the individual mind, the collective mind does not understand the cause of its own suffering. It is ignorant not only of spiritual truth but also the impact of ego. It believes that the answers to the problems of humanity are all 'external' and can be solved by fixing each in turn—usually by force.

As a result, instead of viewing problems as challenges that can only be resolved by changing ourselves on the inside and rising to the next level of consciousness, we look for external culprits and quick solutions. We talk about 'the war on drugs', 'making our country great', 'turning a blind eye to dishonesty for the sake of peaceful relations', 'accepting the "reality" of bribery to win contracts', 'the end justifies the means' or 'that's all part of the game'. We have become so accustomed to the absence of integrity that we have learnt to ignore it and accept it as 'business as usual'. Our collective ego is also more interested in serving itself than in serving the needs of society.

As a result, society is beset by deceptions, half-truths and distortions. It has become difficult to distinguish right from wrong, truth from lie. Many of these manipulations are deliberately designed to pander to man's meanest instincts and make the unacceptable acceptable. Violent computer games are not 'harmless fun' as we are led to believe, but dangerous desensitisers. They deaden the mind to the appalling effects of mindless killing. Social media often cater to the basest emotions and weaknesses of human beings' animal instincts. While both social media and the internet have the capacity to disseminate good, they are more often used for selfish purposes and the pursuit of greed.

False images of happiness and beauty contaminate the minds of the innocent making them feel inadequate and demeaned. Dangerous criminal ideas are projected widely and without compensating commentary, leaving the young with no means of self-protection. Human beings are left unprotected and at the mercy of untruths and dangerous concepts that masquerade as 'social collaboration', 'team spirit', 'religion', 'patriotism', whereas, they sow the seeds of discord.

Almost all human catastrophes have been the result of beliefs, convictions and 'truths' that have been anything but truths. These convictions were just opinions and the perceptions of fallible human beings who used the gullibility of other human beings for their own selfish ego-derived purposes. They have led mankind into the most appalling slaughters, mass killings and repetitive horrors.

At the collective level, it is very important for us not to fall into the same trap when seeking to find solutions to the world's difficult and complex problems. It is too easy to come to ill-considered, rapid conclusions about what needs to be done or, worse still, to replace one negative egoic activity with another. It is too easy to fall into the trap of using violence to achieve results. Hate can never be overcome by hate. It can only be conquered by love.

Effecting change, especially when faced with entrenched opinion, is exceedingly difficult. In the absence of enlightened awareness, the risk is that human beings will keep on repeating the same mistakes and remain unconscious in their reactivity rather than conscious in their response. This is what the Buddha called 'ignorance' and Jesus referred to as 'they know not what they do'. The pressures not to change, the inertia of inaction, the desire to remain inactive and 'comfortable' are very strong. The true evils of our society that must be overcome are ego, ignorance and laziness.

If we are collectively to make the changes we need to ensure the survival of our planet, we must radically change the way we think. We must adopt the practices of an enlightened and more conscious mind. This is the mind of peace, non-violence, tolerance, compassion, kindness, humility and love.

There have been many role models throughout history. Most recently, we have had such luminaries as Mahatma Gandhi, Nelson Mandela, Martin Luther King Jr and Pope John Paul II to name but four. And today, there are millions of less well-known selfless, dedicated and kind people who devote their lives to helping others. They are on the journey of enlightenment and such people will change the world.

The evolution of our collective consciousness has already begun and is growing in force. It is visible everywhere. It is also being met by a growing resistance from forces that benefit from the status quo. These are the forces of 'unconsciousness' and view these changes as threatening and dangerous. This is normal as change always provokes an opposite response. The 'unconscious' must be helped to raise their level of consciousness and awaken to evolve to a new and better world.

Education

Where should we start? As with any change, education is key to addressing the issue of ignorance. When we don't know what we don't know, we cannot improve.

Our education system has been increasingly directed at achieving scores based on academic learning. The sense of worth of schools and teachers is derived from teaching children facts and figures. Less able pupils are often not wanted because they lower the overall result.

This is a consequence of our desire to raise educational standards, which, of itself, is a laudable objective. But it is wholly unsatisfactory when we end up with children who are crammed full of facts but have little awareness of life and few life skills. They may have knowledge, but they lack the capacity to think. The intuition, creativity and sense of wonder that are so essential to life have been all but extinguished. Instead, they have acquired a desire to please by doing what is needed to pass exams—rather than a love of learning and excellence. The resultant selfishness of achievement, which is ego, overwhelms the psyche and becomes the goal of life.

The life-enhancing skills of respect, tolerance, interpersonal understanding and care for others are not part of the curriculum. Gentleness, nurturing, awareness and resilience are not taught. Nor are the practices of collaboration, emotional control, stillness or meditation. Employers find the products of such education very uninspiring and have to re-educate from the beginning.

It has been said that if children from the age of six were taught to find stillness through meditation, the level of anger, violence and bullying would be significantly reduced. This is because such teaching would encourage an understanding of who we are as individuals and our interconnectedness. Knowing this reduces the desire to hurt others.

Despite many valiant efforts to curb it, bullying, both physical and psychological, is rife. Its effect on children (both the bullied and the bullying) is devastating and frequently lifelong. Its effects are felt across the whole of humanity and it is being perpetuated everywhere. Only education will solve it.

We have to teach the understanding that we have both a human and a spiritual dimension and that we are interconnected. Children need to learn what ego is and how to control it. And how to find stillness and peace and how to manage stress must be made part of the education system. Children should be encouraged and helped to meditate and to appreciate the value and benefits of silence, reflection and the discovery of inner peace. At the individual and collective level, we should seek to influence schools, local councils, local authorities and government to include life skills, spiritual teaching and meditation in the curriculum.

Being intelligent is not as important as being wise.

> Knowing others is intelligence;
> knowing yourself is true wisdom.
> Mastering others is strength;
> mastering yourself is true power.
>
> —Lao Tzu, Tao Te Ching, verse 33
> (rendered by Stephen Mitchell)

Parenting

Schools are not the only places of education. Nor are they the most important. A parent or parents are a child's first role-models and they have an immense responsibility for helping their child along the journey of life. What happens in childhood affects our view of the world. One of the most important decisions made by our subconscious mind is whether the world is a friendly or inimical place. This determines many of the attitudes carried into our (and society's) future. Parents have an immense influence on their child's perception of the world. If children are cynical, judgmental, angry, negative and resentful, they are very often reflecting their parents' perspectives.

Because self-gratification is so easy, parents overlook the needs of the child to establish a relationship with them—the most important human beings there are for the child. Opportunities to communicate, share knowledge and above all listen to a child are missed. There is also often the belief that education is the responsibility of the school and not the parent. Nothing could be further from the truth.

Parents also need to be educated so that they can help their child find its way in life. The child needs to learn many things that are not instinctive and need guidance: to take responsibility; to enjoy healthy respectful relationships; to experience the joy of giving as well as receiving; to be humble as well as proud.

In order to do this well, an essential grounding in the life skills we have described is needed. Parents can only teach what they know. If they do not have these skills, they cannot fulfil their most important responsibility. Parents need to have access to sympathetic courses and centres where, without embarrassment, they can learn to help their children in the most productive and loving way.

As we have said, you can only give what you have. It is ultimately up to each parent to develop their level of consciousness to be able to give their child the best start in life. All parents should want their child to be happy by being a decent, loving, compassionate contributor to society. At the individual and collective level, we should encourage local authorities, councils and government to recognise the importance of providing free parenting counselling, in addition to antenatal classes.

Institutions and corporates

It is heartening to see the high level of activities that many institutions and corporates are undertaking in order to create a better life for those they serve and employ. Recently, there has clearly been a much greater level of awareness of important issues such as the environment, well-being at work, probity, transparency and purpose. There are some truly wonderful examples of initiatives and actions in support of creating a better world.

While this is encouraging and entirely right, there is still an enormous way to go. We still see too much box-ticking and lip service in order to appear 'worthy' when the reality is often very different. In the end, it will only be to organisations' benefit to do this well. It is becoming clear that the most talented students are increasingly persuaded to join organisations as much for the values they represent as for the financial benefits. As the complexity of work and the need for skills increases, the battle for talent (both attracting and retaining) intensifies. It is the lifeblood of corporations and the major risk and opportunity facing them.

Corporations are made up of individuals into a collective. If the place of work does not have a soul or a purpose, the individuals will leave their hearts and minds at the door. On the other hand, if the corporation embraces the power of their people and operates in an enlightened and empowering manner, the transformation of both can occur.

This means companies helping employees understand their minds. Whenever possible, they should have competent coaches and mentors. Organisations, both public and private, have a major responsibility and role to play in helping stakeholders and society to evolve towards a higher level of consciousness. Individually and collectively, we can continue to raise the profile of this issue with all stakeholders, influencers, associations and government. If we are investors, we can press to see progress on these matters and decide consciously where to invest. And as customers, we should consider buying from those who best serve our wider needs.

Government

Like institutions, government is made up of people acting both individually and collectively. The *administration* part of government (local and central, state and federal) is responsible for the management of all day-to-day affairs in accordance with law and the instructions of elected officials. Like all institutions, governments are made up of individuals who are expected to act responsibly and with probity. As with those employed in all institutions, these individuals have a major role to play in raising their and others' consciousness to a level capable of meeting the needs of the highly complex challenges that face them. They are often obliged to face conflicting and changing priorities with limited resources. Their role is demanding and highly stressful given the scale and importance of their remit. They are the glue holding things together—even when their environment is in turmoil and the elected officials around them change responsibilities and priorities.

As individuals doing demanding work, they need to learn how to find their inner peace by adopting the guidance here in *The Way*. They also need easy access to well-being and spiritual guidance. This will help them be less reactive and more productive. In their own work, it will help them to differentiate what is and is not essential and what is and is not a priority, as well as the best way to work and collaborate with colleagues who may report to different people or departments. At higher levels—where they interface with difficult, hurried and harried people on the national and international stage—they will be acting from a place of relative calm objectivity and avoid some of the unhealthy consequences of their disjointed life.

The *executive* part of government is responsible for directing the affairs of the country, establishing laws and setting the leadership tone, and is usually done by elected people. If they are not elected, they cannot fulfil their mission, but their election is only the beginning of an opportunity to serve. Theirs is a mission to help make their country (and the world) a better, safer, more harmonious, more tolerant, less dangerous, wealthier, healthier and happier place. At least that is what they are elected to do....

In order to achieve this laudable goal, it is essential that they should understand, be comfortable with and promote the importance of self-discovery, self-control, humility and wisdom. Given the scale of their platform and global visibility, they should be the role models for others to follow. They themselves should be their message. If they cannot grasp the significance of the duality of existence (that we have both a human and spiritual dimension) and if they remain trapped in egoic thinking (image, acclaim and clever sound bites), they will never be able to meet the demands of their electorate. Nor will they enjoy peace. Life will be a continuous source of suffering and disappointment for them and for everyone else. They will never be satisfied. Ego never is.

What is demanded of elected leaders is wisdom, courage, integrity, authenticity. These can only be achieved when human beings know who they are at the deeper, spiritual level. They need to be able to perceive the critical nature of their decisions in the wider context of world peace and the compassionate survival of all who inhabit the planet. There is no room for complacency or arrogance. Leaders should consider seeking the support and help of professional coaches, not to help them with their jobs, but to help them manage stress, manage time, manage their wellbeing and live life. There has never been a greater need for this wisdom.

Leadership

The paragraphs on government, especially executive government, apply equally to leaders of all organisations—big and small— and indeed to *everyone.* Whether we like it or not, we are all leaders to someone. It could be as parent, friend, colleague, partner, collaborator, business leader or simple citizen.

Leadership shows up in the inspired actions of others.

If we accept this statement, we immediately perceive the role we all have in contributing to our society and those we serve—ultimately, all of mankind. We can all inspire someone else and it is one of the joys of life to do so.

As we have explained, 'inspired' comes from the Latin word *spiritus*, meaning breath. So to inspire someone means breathing life into another, stirring their heart and appealing not to the senses but to the soul. Inspiration comes from within. It is formless and from our spiritual dimension. It cannot be seen or touched. Yet it has more power than any form-based instruction or demand.

Great leaders are followed not so much because of what they *do*, but because of who they *are*. This means: what they stand for; the values they demonstrate; the integrity and trust they exude; the belief they have in others and the belief others have in them; their ability to listen; their humility; their acknowledgement of the work of others above their own; their sense of responsibility and the responsibilities they confer on others; their courage to stand up for what is right; their sense of fairness; and their wisdom.

People don't require motivation to act when they are inspired. They are naturally and seamlessly moved to action as if by a spark. It is the spark of awareness and of a growing consciousness. It can change the world.

All of these are qualities of spiritual excellence. They enable leaders to go beyond the confines of ego into a new dimension and a new awareness. A *Harvard Business Review* article published in 2016 based on an assessment of around 50,000 leaders, strongly confirmed the importance of inspiring leadership. The analysis showed that there are many ways to be an inspiring leader, with those able to master multiple approaches—that is, being the most flexible and least rigid—the most effective. The report also showed that, with awareness and help, leaders can learn to become more inspiring. Anyone can do it. *Breathing life into* is a way to stimulate change and find peace in a turbulent world.

> The Master, by residing in the Tao,
> sets an example for all beings.
> Because he doesn't display himself,
> people can see his light.
> Because he has nothing to prove,
> people can trust his words.
>
> —Lao Tzu, Tao Te Ching, verse 22
> (rendered by Stephen Mitchell)

21

Stillness and Peace

The key to finding peace in turbulent times is to find stillness. Stillness is not being stationary, in the sense of motionless inactivity. It is a conscious and alert state of awareness in which we are present in our body and connected to the light of truth. It is a place of peace from which we can become the observers of our thoughts and aware of our awareness. It is who we are at the deepest level. It is a return to our natural state—the place where we are everything, and everything is us.

It is the infinite depth of the ocean while the story of our mortal life happens on the surface. It is the eternal screen on which the film of our life is projected. It is the permanent canvas on which our mortal self, the painter, draws his sketches.

Stillness is space. It is where we realise that we are connected to the Universe and that our mortal body is a short-lived manifestation of our spiritual being. In stillness we learn to come away from the many distractions of our human existence—the noise, stress, emotions, conflicts and time pressures.

Meditation is a wonderful way to access this space and to experience the depth of our being. With practice, we can access that stillness anywhere, even in a crowded, noisy city. We can access it every day in every aspect of our life. And by living life in the foreground and having stillness in the background, the actions we take will be kinder and more considered, compassionate and loving. Life then becomes an opportunity to live in conscious alignment with our truth and, from there, to act from a position of goodness.

While our human form will dissolve and return *to* Source, our spiritual formlessness *is* Source. The trivial anxieties and fears of our daily life cease to have any importance. When we appreciate it is all an unreal and fleeting dream, we awaken into the reality and infinity of consciousness. In stillness there is no fear—even of death. Stillness is peace: eternal and infinite. It is already within us as it always has been.

22

There Is Still Time

There is still time to change the way we think, to resolve the many physical and psychological challenges that humanity faces and to create a better world. There is still time to learn to control ego, the source of so much pain and suffering, and to find peace, even in turbulent and uncertain times.

Although many scientists, tracing the linear progression between where we are and where we are headed, are deeply pessimistic about the ultimate outcome, the authors of this book remain optimistic that human ingenuity, collaboration and creativity, stimulated by the power of heightened consciousness, will find solutions to every challenge.

The solutions are all here in any case. The universe loves to create and grow. As we have said throughout this book, Heaven is inside each one of us. When we rediscover this truth and raise our collective consciousness, we can love our neighbour as our self and create a gentler, more tolerant, more inclusive world. By controlling ego, by dying to our false sense of self and being reborn to who we truly are, the deeper, spiritual, dimension of our presence, we acquire wisdom.

Wisdom is the ultimate Way of truth and peace.

Epilogue

All that we are is the result of what we have thought: it is founded on our thoughts; it is made up of our thoughts. If a man speaks or acts with an evil thought, pain follows him, as the wheel follows the foot of the ox that draws the carriage. All that we are is the result of what we have thought: it is founded on our thoughts; it is made up of our thoughts. If a man speaks or acts with a pure thought, happiness follows him, like a shadow that never leaves him.
The Dhammapada

About the Authors

Vernon Sankey

Vernon Sankey was born in France, educated in the UK and graduated in Modern Languages at Oriel College, Oxford. He went straight from university into industry, where he spent the next 28 years in various countries, culminating as chief executive of a major international corporation headquartered in the UK.

He then became a non-executive director, chairman and advisor of several large and small international companies in France, Switzerland, the UK and the US and is still active in this field today. He has also lectured on leadership, motivation, transformation and personal development at universities, schools and conferences.

In 1999, he co-founded a coaching and mentoring company where he further developed his knowledge of cognitive psychology to help mentor business executives as well as people in all walks of life.

In 2018, he published *The Stairway to Happiness,* which reflects many of the learnings gleaned from his experience as a business leader and coach.

His second book *The Way: Finding Peace in Turbulent Times*, co-authored with Katey Lockwood, takes *The Stairway to Happiness* to new levels.

Vernon is married with four children and six grandchildren and lives in Berkshire.

Katey Lockwood

Katey Lockwood was born and educated in the UK and began her career in media where she worked on the Harry Potter franchise and special effects team.

She studied NLP (neuro linguistic programming) with Richard Bandler and the Kabbalah for a further five years. She then went on to study philosophy at the LSE. During the past decade, she has analysed and studied many philosophical and metaphysical principles, including the Universal Laws and the Hermetica and is also well versed in spiritual practices, including meditation.

Her knowledge of cognitive psychology, philosophy and spirituality has enabled Katey to coach and teach at the highest level. Her list of clients includes business executives, celebrities and high-profile sportspeople as well as those needing help and support in finding a more effective and happier way of conducting their life. Katey also does voluntary work coaching members of the public and friends. She has participated in workshops and discussions on stress management, life skills and personal transformation.

Katey was a trustee of the Katie Piper Foundation, whose vision is to have a world where scars do not limit a person's function, social inclusion or sense of well-being. She worked extensively with Katie.

The Way: Finding Peace in Turbulent Times is Katey's first book, which she is co-authoring with Vernon.

Made in the USA
San Bernardino, CA
02 December 2019

60730803R00160